STAGES OF HEALING

About the authors:

Melissa Steinberg, M.A., is a marriage and family therapist working primarily with adult children of alcoholics. Wendy Joffe, Ph.D., is a psychologist who specializes in addiction and related family issues. Both Steinberg and Joffe work at the Family Life Center in Miami, Florida.

STAGES OF HEALING

A GUIDE FOR COUNSELING
ADULT CHILDREN
OF ALCOHOLICS

Melissa Steinberg, M.A.
and
Wendy Joffe, Ph.D.

First published August 1990.

ISBN: 0-89486-687-7

Library of Congress Catalog Card Number: 90-81554

Printed in the United States of America.

Editor's note:
  Hazelden Educational Materials offers a variety of information on chemical dependency and related areas. Our publi-
cations do not necessarily represent Hazelden or its programs,
nor do they officially speak for any Twelve Step organization.

To my father, Stanley Levien, whose picture of me always included the qualities of creativity, sensitivity, and the ability to write. His wisdom and goodness will always guide me.

— Melissa Steinberg

To my mother, who role modeled for me how to connect with people's heart-space and feelings, and who inspired me into the profession of psychology.

— Wendy Joffe

Contents

Acknowledgments

The authors would like to acknowledge the support, input, feedback, and wealth of knowledge that was so generously given by the following special persons:

Dave Hudson, for his expertise in storytelling and construction of metaphors.

Leon Matsil, for the magnanimous use of his personal computer and office, as well as his ongoing patient and limitless instruction in the use of the computer.

Bonnie and Rick Levenson, for their feedback, assistance, and love.

Our families, for their tolerance, flexibility, encouragement, and undying belief and pride in us.

Our patients, who provided us experience and taught us about courage, strength, resiliency, and resourcefulness.

A Note to the Readers

The facts and observations presented in this book regarding adult children of alcoholics are tendencies that the authors have observed in their therapeutic practice. The authors, however, recognize that this population of patients can exhibit a variety of exceptional qualities that should be recognized and affirmed.

The case histories in this book are based on many individuals. Any resemblance to one person is purely coincidental.

Introduction

Mary: *I've been in therapy for years, and I can't do that right either. I try and try, and no matter what I do nothing changes.*

Therapist: *What have you tried?*

Mary: *I try to be what everybody wants me to be, but it's never good enough.*

Therapist: *What do you mean by "everybody"?*

Mary: *Every guy I meet treats me like garbage. It doesn't matter how much I do for my good daddy.*

Therapist: *Who's your "good daddy"?*

Mary: *My therapist told me to stop being angry with my father, 'cause that's why I was picking all these crummy men. She told me to stop thinking about what happens with my family and to take a close look at myself.*

Therapist: *Do you know why you're so angry with your father?*

Mary: *You don't want me to get into that, do you? Every time I told my other therapist about my father's fits, she told me to stop living in the past. He still has fits, but she told me his fits shouldn't affect me 'cause I don't live with him anymore.*

Therapist: *Your father has fits?*

Mary: *Yeah, fits. He'll get angry and yell and sometimes throw things, but Mom keeps telling me it's no big deal and that he's really sorry for what he's done.*

Therapist: *It sounds like your dad can sometimes get out of control. Would he tend to have his fits after he'd been drinking alcohol?*

Mary: *Yeah, all the time. How'd you know? But then, drinking is pretty normal, right?*

Therapist: *How often did your dad drink?*

Mary: *Every day.*

Therapist: *We'll have to explore it further, but it sounds like your dad may be an alcoholic.*

Mary: *Is that important?*

This dialogue may seem all too familiar. Real change does not occur for any adult unless core issues are looked at. Knowing how to help the patient work through the impact of his or her family of origin is critical for the therapist in general practice. This is particularly true for persons who have experienced childhood traumas, as is the case of children raised with an alcoholic parent.

As colleagues, we have worked a total of twenty-five years in the field of psychological service. We commonly consult with one another on cases. Several years ago we began to see a pattern in our patients' profiles and saw that we weren't getting the results we wanted. Patients came to see us with family or relationship issues. Although their present lives appeared "successful," they were overwhelmed by current problems. Our psychological training and treatment approach had been directive and structural-strategic.

Because we felt stuck, we decided to broaden our perspective and style. We started to question our patients' past and asked about their personal histories. The more questions we asked, the more we heard themes of alcoholism: deprivation, emotional neglect, physical abuse, and sexual abuse. These themes, though not indicative only to adult children of alcoholics, appeared more pronounced, more consistently in conjunction with one another, and more frequently than with other patient populations. We became curious. Are there unique qualities to this population? Do they require a special understanding and different methods of intervention in order for them to experience psychological healing?

We began to educate ourselves about the disease of alcoholism. We studied reading material, attended Adult Children of Alcoholics and Al-Anon meetings, talked to professionals working with chemically dependent people and their families, and attended professional workshops. Most importantly, we explored and discussed the aspects and ramifications of the disease with our patients themselves. The answer to our questions became apparent. We learned that the effects of alcoholism were at the very core of our patients' difficulties and current stresses.

In talking with other clinicians in a general private practice, we found they too were discovering a vast majority of patients who were at some point in their lives impacted by alcoholism. We all wondered if this was a new phenomena, or had we all missed the mark by not asking the questions that would uncover alcoholism? Like us, our colleagues felt a need to acquire skills and tools that would help this population. The vast majority of reading material and professional training focused on the identification of adult children of alcoholics as a diagnostic group, but failed to offer concrete recovery strategies.

We found that almost all of those who either presented or attended professional conferences and workshops on alcoholism identified themselves as adult children of alcoholics or as family members of alcoholics. It became apparent that therapists who themselves were affected by alcoholism were sensitive to those of their patients who shared that experience. As clinicians who did not have a significant relationship with an alcoholic in our past or present, we were definitively in the minority. The totality of our learning about alcoholism reinforced our belief that clinicians (whether affected by alcoholism or not) need to develop their sensitivity to adult children of alcoholics and codependency. Most clinical psychological training does not define or discuss alcoholism. Yet the disease is pervasive, and its impact is significant on our patient population.

As a result, we developed a specialization in helping people affected by alcoholism, particularly adult children of alcoholics. We have taken a broad and eclectic approach. We have amalgamated all that we have learned with all the tools and techniques that we have created and successfully implemented and produced this book. We hope to offer the therapeutic community not only the ability to identify the impact of addiction, but the successful means to help their patients ameliorate the pain caused by childhood trauma.

For us, the process of sharing, brainstorming, and providing support for one another while treating the adult children of alcoholics population has been invaluable. It is our intent not only to offer methods to effect positive change, but also to encourage clinicians to use our formulations as a springboard to expand their own creativity and knowledge — both with their patients and with their colleagues.

CHAPTER ONE

General Theoretical Framework

The disease of alcoholism is defined as follows:

1. A need to drink alcohol, versus a desire to do so.
2. An inability by the person to stop drinking alcohol, or the inability to control the amount or frequency of intake.
3. The drinking of alcoholic beverages impedes the person's social and family relationships or occupational functioning.
4. Alcohol is a priority in the person's life above all else.
5. The dependence upon alcohol is both physiological and psychological.

An Adult Child of an Alcoholic (ACOA) is an adult who grew up with an alcoholic in the parental role. The impact of alcoholism during childhood affects this person as he or she matures into adulthood. Being raised in an alcoholic family contributes to the problems he or she experiences as an adult. The disease affects adult children in the following areas:

• Their belief systems
• The rules that build the structure of their relationships
• Their self-perception and identity
• Their personal sense of impact on the world
• Their developmental process
• It limits their emotional identification and expression

The effects of alcoholism and the resultant personal and interpersonal patterns are passed on like a legacy from generation to generation if effective intervention doesn't occur.

TRAITS OF ADULT CHILDREN OF ALCOHOLICS

Children in alcoholic families experience many traumas. Their parents or significant adults are not there to act as buffers or in a manner that validates them. The adults are not there to help them work through their feelings or understand their experiences. As a result, these children may become emotionally blocked and stuck in their quandary. As they age and mature, they may repeat and rehearse the feelings evoked in past, personal traumas, unconsciously seeking resolution. Just as addictive behaviors and compulsions can have a hereditary quality, so do unresolved traumas. In our work we have found that when adult children of alcoholics become parents, these unresolved traumas can be passed down via fears, distorted perceptions, and overreactive responses.

Disassociating from Feelings

We believe that many adult children of alcoholics are experts at distracting themselves, at disassociating from their feelings. They have learned that they cannot get their needs met, so they put their feelings on hold. They believe it is safer to be numb than to be vulnerable. It is impossible, though, to shut out selected feelings. One feels or one doesn't. Not feeling protects a person from grieving or pain, but it also hinders the process of attachment, love, or intimacy. Though chronologically many adult children of alcoholics appear ready for a commitment, developmentally they may still be in their childhood with the crises that occurred. In a lot of ways, many of the patients we treat are like children: needy, narcissistic, without an identity, emotionally raw, and with undeveloped defenses. The lack of interpersonal boundaries and the association of love with pain create enormous obstacles to a rewarding relationship.

Growing up in an alcoholic family can mean growing up with extremes. Rules are rigid. Feelings are either repressed or explosive. Relationships are peripheral or enmeshed. The familial tone can be either one of tension or active crisis. Extremes in the environment may lead to extremes in response. This encourages extremes in process and thinking. Many adult children of alcoholics tend to think dichotomously: black or white, all or nothing. As children, they may mask the family's problems with a happy face and a perfect facade. If they're not perfect, then they're bad. They may judge themselves harshly. They may deny problems, difficulties, or weaknesses to themselves and to others. Not being able to handle everything is not being able to handle anything at all. One mistake may have the power to erase any accomplishment.

Barbara, the younger by two years, and her brother Shawn grew up with an alcoholic father. Shawn was labeled by the family as the problem child. His behavior aroused severe criticism, anger, attention, and blame from his parents. When Mother and Father were not yelling at Shawn, they were fighting — sometimes violently — with one another. Through observation of family interactions, Barbara quickly learned that there were enormous consequences to even the smallest mistakes. She wished she was invisible. She prayed for total perfection.

To cope, Barbara emotionally disengaged from her family and physically isolated herself from them as much as possible. She was not nurtured, and she chose neglect over abuse. To the outside world, Barbara played the role of the perfect child. She believed if she was perfect, she would be safe and gain control over her life. Any error wrought her with anxiety and terror. As she matured, she developed a success-or-failure approach to living. All facets of her life were held up to scrutiny. Barbara's unrealistically high expectations of herself and her life created an unrelenting and reinforcing image of herself as a failure.

Many adult children of alcoholics don't trust their feelings, perceptions, or desires. They learn as children that being free and spontaneous may evoke pain in themselves and others. They believe when they take care of themselves, they discount others. As children, they learn to numb their own needs and feelings. To fill the void, they develop antennae to accurately read and anticipate everyone else's needs and feelings. They learn to be reactors and internalize a strong sense of responsibility for those around them. They live for everyone else.

Loyalty and Fear of Betrayal

Adult children's low self-esteem and mistrust of their own perceptions may lead to an overinvolvement and unconditional commitment to the significant people in their lives. This is learned at a very early age in response to the relationship with their parents. The sober parent becomes idealized. Children see that parent as the only source of security they have, even though neither parent may be emotionally available to them.

Children protect their relationship with their parents. They never want to risk rejection by airing negative or hostile feelings. They develop a blind sense of loyalty, forever protecting against their fear of abandonment. Just as the alcoholic parent denies he or she is an alcoholic, the children deny the presence and impact of the disease. To contend with this situation, children emotionally shut down. This "shut down" protects them from emotional pain, from feeling their own anger, and from betraying the alcoholic and the alcoholic family system.

Fear of Rejection, Abandonment, Confrontation, Anger

An umbrella of fear shields all of an adult child's emotions. This fear immobilizes many adult children from feeling and acting on their feelings. The fear originates in infancy, when even from that time, there's an awareness of a lack of stability in the family. Security blooms from structure, consistency, predictability, emotional and physical dependability, and safety. It develops from a knowledge that love is given in order to nurture the child rather than to serve the parents' needs. It grows from a belief that one's needs will be cared for and attended to. When these qualities are not present, life is erratic. This familial atmosphere encourages children to seek immediate gratification, as it is unknown what will happen from one moment to the next. What is real, what is promised now, may be denied or taken away five minutes later. Fear grows out of this lack of security and safety.

We've found that many adult children internalize their lack of nurturance because they assume they are not worthy. They perceive that their needs will not be met. They fear abandonment or punishment for just wanting. Because of their dependence on their parents, they blame themselves for wanting too much or wanting the wrong thing. They respond by not trusting their own feelings, and they depend on others to define and validate them.

> Gwen's parents were both addicts: her mother was addicted to prescription drugs; her father to alcohol. Her mother was prone to bouts of depression, at which time she would stay in bed, sometimes for weeks. Her father would vacillate between violent rages and states of dependence, neediness, and affection. Like every child, Gwen relied on her parents to provide care, love, and security. When her parents, due to their own problems, turned on her or away from her, Gwen blamed herself. Gwen questioned her every action and always drew the same conclusion: she was responsible. "If only I stayed home from school, Dad wouldn't have gotten drunk.... If I didn't tell Mom I was hungry, she wouldn't have gotten upset, taken those pills, and gone to bed."

> *Gwen grew to believe that in order for everyone else to be safe, and for her to get some semblance of love, she could not need. To keep some order and balance in her life, Gwen decided she had to repress her needs and feelings. She believed she was not deserving, and she felt extremely uncomfortable and mistrusting of anything positive said, given, or offered to her.*

According to patients who have grown up in an alcoholic family, it becomes terrifying to just be, to feel, or to express one's feelings. This fear is distorted, magnified. If any feeling is expressed in an alcoholic family, it's anger (and it's usually expressed in an overreactive, uncontrollable, and often violent manner). Feeling, then, is equated with anger, and anger is equated with rage. Rage paints a terrifying picture of self-destruction, destroying others, annihilation, or total abandonment.

Many adult children's fear of rejection, abandonment, confrontation, or anger dominates their personal and interpersonal needs. They may grow to believe that neither themselves nor their needs are important. Silently acknowledging and protecting their fear has a more predictable outcome than risking acknowledgment and verbalization of the need. Though the fear is uncomfortable, it is familiar. The resultant anxious energy becomes an integral part of their lives, giving them permission to observe and analyze life, rather than actively participating in it.

> *In session, Karen, an adult child of an alcoholic father, talks about her feeling of constant dread. "In the morning, just as my eyes open, I become aware of this heavy weight on my chest. I think of what I need to do that day, and my chest tightens. 'What if I forget that?' . . . 'What if I mess that up?' . . . 'What if he gets mad at me?' The drive to get it all done and the fear that I won't propel me out of bed. I spend my day vigilantly scanning for the 'boogeyman' — you know, the problem that inevitably has to happen. There's almost a comfort when something*

finally goes wrong. If by the time I go to bed at night and nothing bad has happened, I become terrified. I lay there knowing I messed up, and I just didn't see it. There's nothing worse than knowing, sooner or later, you're going to get caught."

Identity: Caretaking and Narcissism

A childhood defined by chaotic and extreme behavior often breeds a child with extremes in self-perception. Many adult children either define themselves by totally meeting everyone else's needs while sacrificing their own, or by being completely self-involved, seeking only self-preservation. They believe that their existence is either for others or for themselves, fearing that otherwise, they will become nonentities. In either case, there is a complete detachment from their own feelings and wants.

Adult children who look to others to define themselves feel powerless over themselves and their own lives. Conversely, because they endure to be the caretakers of others, they may feel all-powerful over the lives of their significant others. They believe they possess omnipotent, catastrophic abilities over their loved ones. If something negative has happened or may happen to someone they love, no matter how removed or how remote, adult children may take it on as their fault, their responsibility.

Ken grew up with an alcoholic mother and a passive, peripheral father. Ken tried his best to be a "good boy": do all the chores, maintain a happy face, entertain his mother, and get good grades in school. He was convinced if he was wonderful enough, his father would notice him and his mother wouldn't drink. He was sure that he had the ability to control their moods and behavior.

Ken tells the story of one tragic day when he was eleven years old. "I overslept and was running late for school. I knew if I did the breakfast dishes, I would miss

> *the bus. I made the decision to take care of the dishes when I got home from school that afternoon. When I got home, I found my mom sprawled out on the living room floor, unconscious, and bleeding from shattered glass. I just knew it was my fault. If only I was more responsible. If only I hadn't made all those wrong decisions in the morning. If I wasn't so stupid, my mother would have been all right."*

In our practice we have found that, like caretaking adult children, narcissistic adult children also feel powerless over their world and the people in it. They pretend to be totally self-sufficient and independent. Their sense of self is so ill-defined, they fear losing themselves in someone else if they get emotionally close. If a significant relationship ends, they may feel virtually annihilated. It takes all their psychic energy to try to maintain this "I don't need anybody" facade. It is lonely, but safe. As a result, they function feeling isolated. Because they make sure that no one needs them and that they don't need anyone else, they also feel they have no impact, no place, and no control over anyone or anything in their environment.

Sibling Bond

We believe each individual in an alcoholic family grows up in isolation. There is a bond of secrecy between the siblings. The children are taught not to discuss the drinking, to deny that a parent is drinking, and to distrust their perceptions. This is covertly or overtly communicated between family members. This "don't talk" rule operates between those within and outside the family. Most family members wear a mask of normalcy in and out of the family home. Its purpose is to cover the mistrust, pain, low self-esteem, fear, and vulnerability felt by its wearer. It also blocks any possibility of an emotional or interpersonal connection. As a result of not talking, each sibling harbors his or her own, often skewed, picture of childhood experiences.

Greta and Lola are sisters, raised with an alcoholic, abusive father and a very busy, socially active, but emotionally distant mother. Since childhood, and way into adulthood, Greta and Lola have held the perception that their parents purposely placed a wedge between them. Greta and her mother were repeatedly and brutally beaten by the father. Lola was spared the father's physical abuse, and consequently, emotionally aligned with him. The more Greta was physically and emotionally abused by her father, the more her resentment and hatred for Lola grew.

Lola had some awareness that her sister was being hurt by her father, but only to a minimal degree. Lola needed to insulate herself from the pain her sister was going through in order to maintain the emotional bond she had with her father. The bond is what Lola believed kept her physically safe.

Later, as adults, the sisters began discussing their childhood. Greta confronted her sister, stating, "Not only did you not get beaten by Father, you got his love!" Lola rebutted Greta's perceptions with, "You're right. I didn't get beatings, but I also got little else. Father took me places all right, but places where he would sit and drink. I was in a neutral spot, and I did everything I could to safeguard that position. I ignored your pain, Greta, for my own survival."

Within sibling relationships, extremes are again found. Usually the eldest is overinvolved, attempting to replace what is perceived as a lack of parenting of the other siblings. This role serves to rescue both the children and the parents. The alternative is a rivalrous and polarized relationship between siblings. This stems from interpreting one or both parents' attentions, even those that are negative or hostile, as favoritism for the other sibling. When children feel unloved and rejected by either one or both of their parents, they may react to parent-sibling interaction with jealousy and self-recrimination.

A major shift occurs when these siblings begin to talk with one another. As they share their individual experiences, they no longer feel so isolated or "crazy." Their talks confirm their perceptions and their reality. It acts as the first step toward developing empathy for one another, as well as a relationship based on truth and understanding. As the sibling roles change, they learn to be there for one another in more genuine and loving ways. They become more emotionally accessible to each other, establish clearer boundaries between them, and slowly let go of the dysfunctional parts they played (caretaker, pseudo-parent, protector, rival, competitor, scapegoat).

Steven and Mary, as young children, emotionally disengaged themselves from one another. As a child, Mary was aligned with her father, seeing him as the innocent victim of her mother's alcoholic behavior. She became her father's confidante, his "substitute" wife. In exchange, Mary's father provided her with nurturance and warmth.

There was a heavy cost. Mary feared if she didn't devote herself to her father and give him all of her attentions, she would get nothing from him. She socially isolated herself and turned to her father to meet all of her emotional needs. She fiercely guarded their relationship, not wanting to share him with her brother Steven. Steven hated his sister and was intensely jealous of the attention she received from their father. His mother's involvement in his life was unreliable and inconsistent, but it was all that Steven felt he had. Their parents' marital conflicts and the roles they played when they fought only fostered Mary's protective stance and Steven's withdrawal.

As adults, Steven and Mary grew even further apart. After their mother died, Mary continued to protect and foster her close relationship with her father. When her father remarried, Mary felt a deep sense of loneliness and emptiness. When her father chose someone else to take care of him, she felt as if she had lost her purpose in life. She realized she had no identity of her own.

Steven, too, was feeling lonely, but this was a familiar feeling he had long ago labeled as isolation. Steven had for years medicated his own pain with alcohol, but was now in recovery. He felt ready to start talking about his childhood with his sister. Steven and Mary visited with one another. Gradually, after much honest and open sharing, they each realized how their parents' behavior greatly contributed to their separation. They became aware that they could provide each other with the balance, support, and nurturance they were missing in their lives. A bridge between them started to be built. They were not alone; they had each other.

Through honest communication, many adult children gain more awareness and insight into their childhood. With this knowledge, they begin to move away from self-blame to self-forgiveness. They can also develop an understanding of their family constellation, their behavior, and its consequences. In risking a more intimate relationship with their siblings, they gain a new definition of love and human connection. This opens the door to an alternative way to interact, a new foundation upon which to build a mutually enhancing and trusting relationship outside of their family of origin.

Parenting: Dealing with Emotional Deprivation

When many adult children become parents, they struggle to avoid their parents' dysfunctional responses, but they see their own childhood pain and fear in their children's eyes. They want to express closeness, bonding, and love to their children, but they don't know how. They did not have effective role models. They did not learn how to emotionally give and receive. They did not learn how to nurture or how to appropriately tend to someone else's needs. They learned, instead, how to disassociate from their feelings in order to cope with their pain. Many adult children unwittingly perpetuate the alcoholic family system, regardless of their yearning for something else. This internal, emotional "tug-of-war" exacerbates the self-blame the adult children already feel. It increases the amount of self-punitive beliefs and the depth of their emotional pain.

As a child, Brittany learned that she could not trust her parents to be there for her. Her mother was alcoholic, and her father was very caught up in her mother's disease. Neither of her parents had much time left for Brittany. She learned to keep to herself and to expect nothing from others. She chose superficial relationships over the possibility of disappointment or rejection.

As an adult, Brittany numbed away her need for others with the use of cocaine. Her addiction and her fears flourished in the face of marriage and parenthood. In her late thirties, Brittany hit bottom and began her recovery process. She had an enormous amount of material to sort out around her childhood — so much so, that she frequently confused her own experience with that of her children's. Their behavior and reactions to her would trigger unresolved feelings and issues that she had with her own parents. Coping with the overwhelming wave of her own responses took precedence over meeting the needs of her children.

The more Brittany withdrew, the more desperate her children became for her attention. Their despondency paralyzed her with fear and filled her with guilt. She felt inadequate and incapable of being the dependable and loving parent she knew they so vitally needed.

Many adult children who seek out therapy are emotionally very needy; developmentally, they may be like children. When they become parents, they have difficulty separating their own needs from their children's needs. Their own emotional deprivation prevents them from being able to provide their children with the unconditional love and support their children need. These patients may respond to their children not for who they are in the present, but in terms of their own experiences as children in the past. Adult children tend to unconsciously reproduce the same pain in their children that they experienced, though the method may be different. After each historically repetitive incident, these parents have great sensitivity to their children's enormous emotional hurt. They respond by internalizing much guilt and self-degradation.

> *Jennifer was victim to her father's verbal and physical abuse whenever he was on an alcoholic binge. As an adult, she still harbors much anger and hurt at her father for his hostile and abusive behavior. Her unresolved pain from childhood gets acted out in abusive interactions with her own children. She finds herself treating her own children as her father treated her. Jennifer feels enormous guilt after these episodes, as she clearly knows the horror of being a victim. Her shame and self-blame eat away at her self-esteem and her perceptions of herself as a mother.*

When adult children become parents, it may be difficult for them to avoid their own issues. They see themselves in their children, and this often forces them to deal with their own childhood experiences. They will have a rush of feelings that for years had been suppressed. The feelings that surface are difficult to sort out, identify, or understand. In order to survive as children, they repressed the sensation and expression of their emotions. As parents, they tend to respond to their children with many of their pent-up emotions, particularly frustration and anger. In turn, they try to shut off their children's emotional response to them. Hence, one part of the cycle is perpetuated.

Seeing that all too familiar pain in their children's eyes often motivates parents who are adult children to change.

> *Shelley was emotionally deprived by her alcoholic mother. Once she had children, she was determined not to treat them as her mother treated her. Despite her resolu-*

tion, Shelley felt herself distancing from her children, particularly her daughter.

During the day, Shelley busied herself with various personal interests and activities. In the evenings, when the family was together, she became easily irritated by the children. Her daughter received the brunt of the hostility, with much yelling and assigned blame directed to her. Shelley recognized her inability to nurture and get close to her daughter. She felt horrible; she knew her daughter needed her, yet she responded to her daughter with the same negativity, criticism, and avoidance that her mother subjected her to.

Shelley's discomfort with her own rejecting behavior motivated her to get help. The impetus to enter therapy for herself was not enough, but her sensitivity to the probable anguish her daughter was experiencing propelled her into treatment.

Individual psychotherapy helps such patients emotionally relive the past and work through it. The therapeutic issues may be between these parents and their children, but the source is within the adult child's family of origin. Through individual therapy, adult children open themselves up to their pasts. The more they grow to understand themselves, the more they are able to differentiate themselves from their children. They cease to relate as children to their children but, instead, as mature adults. As adult children of alcoholics are freed from the blame for their childhood, they begin to take responsibility for themselves and their children. As these parents learn to identify and acknowledge what they need, they become more available to satisfy the needs of their children.

Intimacy: The Familiar Feeling of Being Unworthy of Love

The theme of extremes also exists within intimate relationships. In the initial stage of a "coupling" relationship (whether an adult child or not), it is not unusual for the partners to be powerfully and emotionally enmeshed. Thoughts such as, *He is my everything. . . . I don't need anyone but her. . . . She is everything I need* are common sentiments. Generally these feelings temper, and the couple becomes more realistic about their interpersonal fulfillment.

For many, however, these feelings don't diminish; they continue. The initial enmeshment is their definition of intimacy. The relationship acts as a substitute for their lack of self-definition. The boundaries between themselves and others are blurred. The enmeshment continues until they become aware that their partner cannot totally fill them up. Such patients may conclude that if their partner cannot be and give *everything*, then their partner cannot offer *anything*. The ensuing disappointment leads to feelings of personal rejection, pain, and self-blame. At this point, these adult children may either emotionally disengage from their partner or vainly struggle to change their partner into becoming their everything. The isolation and futility of their actions perpetuates the cycle of self-blame and feelings of failure and worthlessness.

> *Beth, an adult child, is married to Ron. During a therapy session, Beth recounts an interaction between her and Ron the night prior to her last trip home to see her family. "I was extremely anxious. I felt nauseous. I couldn't eat a thing, and I desperately needed Ron's reassurance. Much to my dismay, Ron was experiencing his own nervous anxieties. We had to go on an airplane the next day, and he's terrified of flying. He was perspiring and feeling light-headed and dizzy. All I could think of was,* How dare he not be okay when I need him so badly?*
>
> I quickly went to work trying to fix him. I told him to sit down with his head between his knees; I told him to lie down, to drink juice, to do deep breathing. Nothing I told him worked. The more attention I gave him, the worse he felt. I was terrified. I didn't think I'd get through the*

night if he wasn't going to be strong and supportive of me. I began to think that Ron was purposely getting sick, that he really didn't want to be there for me to begin with. No one was ever there for me before; why should someone be there now? I felt so alone and despicable. I took medication to settle my stomach and cried myself to sleep.

Sociologically, women are given greater permission than men to own and emote their feelings. Female adult children who seek therapeutic help may appear more articulate and verbal about their feelings, but it is usually on a superficial level. These women may tend to look to men to define them. They usually respond to family alcoholism by internalizing the blame, believing they are responsible. Outside the family they adapt by believing they can control the people in their environment through nurturing and caretaking behaviors. In intimate relationships, they may reach out and take care of others in an attempt to protect their own vulnerability, affirm their worthiness, and insure their partner's need for them.

Joan was devastated by the unpredictability of her father's behavior due to his alcoholism. When he was sober, he was warm and sensitive. When he drank, he was hostile, punitive, and critical. Each time he came home she wondered which father she would be seeing. Joan dealt with his erratic personality changes by trying to make everything at home as nice as possible. She thought if she was good, if she could please him, then maybe she could control which father would be with her. Joan convinced herself that if she was "enough," her father would not need to drink. Conversely, if her father drank, she felt it was due to her own failing.

As an adult, Joan continued to try to control her environment by taking care of everything and everyone. At her job she was on every committee. Joan's friends all knew that if they ever had a problem, Joan would be their first call as she was always readily available for them. Being in control and needed also had a side benefit: it safeguarded Joan from receiving. Joan learned as a child that just wanting from others was hurtful. To open up and need would leave her vulnerable to disappointment and self-blame. To appear to herself and others as indefatigable and indefectible meant preservation to her.

Male adult children, as well as addicts who are adult children, also tend to internalize the blame for the family alcoholism. They don't, however, feel that their behavior has a direct impact on others. Their pain seems to come from perceiving themselves as the cause of their parents' drinking, yet being helpless to stop it. They feel they are "bad" and protect this "bad seed" image by either overcompensating and overachieving, or by acting out this image to the extreme. Consequently, they often push away and test their partner in order to protect themselves from being found out and rejected. For these adult children, there is safety in emotional distance. Instead of looking to their partner to define them, they will search outside the relationship to more objective and external successes to accomplish the same end.

Carl was raised by an alcoholic father and a passive, dependent mother. His father was dogmatic and held unachievable and inconsistent expectations of Carl and his sister Yvonne. For Carl's father, no one could give enough or be enough to satisfy him. When he has had his fill of frustration, his father would leave for several days — sometimes weeks — without telling the family his whereabouts. Carl remembers his early childhood years as wrought with confusion and tension. The family atmosphere was like a heavy blanket of depression that none of them felt capable of throwing off.

Once Carl entered grade school, a coach discovered a wonderful gift of Carl's — he was a terrific athlete, particularly in baseball. Carl recollects this time as a turning point in his life. He had a purpose and a place to get recognition and support. He gained a role model and an escape, both emotionally and physically, from his family.

Carl, even as a youngster, became driven to be a baseball star at the sacrifice of all else. In his teen years he became compulsively self-disciplined: no alcohol, no drugs, no dating, lots of rest, healthy eating habits, a limited social life. Baseball became his coping skill. He had a persona and a viable way to keep his family and the world at a safe distance.

Carl's goal was to be accepted as a professional player on a major league team. He was determined that baseball was his destiny. Carl's hard work was to be rewarded. When he graduated from high school, Carl tried out for a minor league team and was hired with much enthusiasm by the team's staff. Carl knew he was on his way. It was only a matter of time before the majors' scouts would see him and scoop him up as one of their own.

Carl was on the team for one year before tragedy struck. An injury to his shoulder shattered his dreams and his life's focus. He was told he could never play professional ball again. He was alone, without an identity, without friends, without skills, and without hope. He felt he was the failure he fought so hard not to be and the person his father had repeatedly told him he was.

The coping styles of both male and female adult children may result in much self-absorption. They utilize a lot of energy to protect against rejection and to defend their vulnerabilities. Their energy is not available to give unconditionally in developing, strengthening, and nurturing relationships. Their intimacy needs are ultimately not met as they are more involved in building and maintaining a protective persona than in building and maintaining a relationship.

The adult child's dichotomous belief system tends to operate within interpersonal rules and roles. There is a pervasive rigidity: one is the receiver, one is the giver; one is in control, one is submissive; one makes all the decisions, one acquiesces; one partner's needs are acknowledged, one partner minimizes and sacrifices his or her needs. Within such a closed and inflexible belief system, neither person in the relationship has the opportunity to be fulfilled.

Adult children tend to select partners who will collude in maintaining this familiar rigidity. They will frequently and repeatedly choose partners who cannot give them the nurturance, acceptance, and love they so desperately need. As children, they personalized their parents' neglect and rejection of them as being their fault. They rationalized that they were to blame, and that they deserved no more than what they received. As adults, adult children of alcoholics are more likely to seek partners who are withholding or rejecting. If they can change their partner into someone who validates them, adult children believe they will then be relinquished of the self-blame and sense of failure they feel from believing they're unworthy of being loved.

Gena was physically abused by her alcoholic father during most of her childhood. She doesn't remember any warm or loving interactions with him. She grew up feeling unworthy of love, particularly of a man's love. For a partner, Gena chose Aaron, also an adult child. Like her father, he was critical, rejecting, and had difficulty expressing tenderness or caring. In fact, affection only occurred if preceded by a fight or some form of hostile exchange. Again, the familiar feeling of being unworthy of love was there.

Gena decided that if she could get Aaron into therapy and successfully influence him to open up, Aaron would be able to change and love her as she wanted to be loved. She believed it was her responsibility and her task to facilitate the atmosphere under which Aaron would become accepting and nurturing. Aaron agreed to go to marital therapy, but continued to be verbally abusive and to initiate the same negative patterns. Gena interpreted her marital inertia as her failure alone. She resolved to end therapy and stay in the relationship, fearing that she really did not deserve to be loved and would never find anyone to meet her needs.

CONCLUSION

Alcoholism is a family disease that traumatizes each member. The children learn to disassociate from their feelings and needs in order to cope with the pain. The rigidity and dysfunction of the family system impedes the children's development of self-worth. Their low self-esteem breeds insecurity and fear of abandonment by those they love. Adult children tend to carry the effects of their childhood into adulthood. The rules, beliefs, and communication patterns of their families of origin are the foundation upon which they build new relationships. No matter how agonizing, they behave, respond, and interpret the world in the same familiar way as they did with their family. Though what they do doesn't work, it's all they know.

Adult children present a complex puzzle to the clinician. When these patients enter therapy, they bring with them their whole family histories. Their families of origin play a critical and active part in who these adult children are and the problems they are experiencing in their present lives. The many facets of adult children and their treatment can be overwhelming for the clinician. While concentrating primarily on the milieu of individual psychotherapy, we offer in the succeeding chapters a wellspring of information and techniques from which the clinician can draw to successfully intervene.

Why Individual Psychotherapy?

There are various modalities, some of which will be touched upon in this book, in which adult children can successfully change. The focus here, however, will be on strategies to be implemented in individual psychotherapy.

Adult children can be experts at keeping their emotions secret, both from themselves and others. Due to the excessive emotional pain they experienced as children, they learned to numb and lock away their feelings. Feelings connoted vulnerability, danger, and rejection. The more adult children are detached from their feelings, the more detached they are from their identity. Their lacking sense of self causes them to look to others to define them. Boundaries are ill-defined; it is, at best, blurry as to where they end and others begin. Boundary issues interfere with adult children's ability to take responsibility for themselves. This facilitates their tendency to blame and focus on others.

Interactionally, consistent themes of minimizing, denial, fear of disloyalty, fear of confrontation, and fear of rejection can exist. Adult children can have difficulty trusting themselves and others. They need to be honest with themselves before they can be honest with others. Individual psychotherapy helps adult children confront and center on themselves. They learn to own and embrace their feelings, perceptions, and life experiences. Once this is accomplished, they are then more capable of fully utilizing alternative therapeutic milieus, such as marital, family, and group.

The therapist is an anchor person who provides a trusting bond and foundation for the patient. This solid human element provides a safe testing ground for adult children to risk expressing feelings, experiment with new beliefs and behaviors, and experience their personal impact on the world. The therapeutic relationship evolves as therapy progresses. Where there was a void for the patient interpersonally, adult children in individual psychotherapy find a person in the therapist who is unconditional, accessible, and validating.

CHAPTER TWO

Assessment Process

Sometimes, a patient will come into the office stating that he or she is an adult child of an alcoholic and wanting to work on these issues. More frequently, however, these patients will present a different problem, seemingly unrelated to the alcoholism that has touched their lives.

The alcoholic family system's dysfunction dictates minimizing, denial, secrecy, fear of betrayal, and extreme loyalty in order to cope with the system and its members. As a result, adult children can be far removed from their origin of pain. In addition, they have learned to mask their pain and problems behind a facade of attempted perfection. They have been — directly and indirectly — punished for having any difficulties. Problems are equated with being a "bad person." Adult children will tend to deny difficulties even to their therapists, not wanting to appear "bad" to them. They may minimize or deny in the therapeutic setting to safeguard against anticipated rejection. Because of the strength of these learned coping skills, the clinician needs to be an astute investigator.

COMMON PROBLEMS OF ADULT CHILDREN

Though this list is not all inclusive, these are the most commonly presented problems adult children bring to the clinician.

- Depression
- Sexual dysfunction

- Eating disorders
- Compulsive behaviors
- Violence
- Free-floating anxiety
- Alcohol or other drug abuse
- Inability to establish and maintain satisfying relationships
- Parenting difficulties
- Phobias
- Lack of identity, direction, goals

These issues presented by adult children are not necessarily different from the issues presented by patients seen in a general private practice. Theirs are just intensified. The patterns created in alcoholic families are similar and overlap with those seen in many dysfunctional families where alcoholism is not present.

Profiles of Adult Children

The pain of growing up in a home touched by alcoholism manifests itself in a variety of forms. In general, there are several typical profiles of an adult child. None of the profiles are exclusive, and they may interweave or change within an adult child's life. But children in alcoholic families do tend to adapt by taking on one of the following roles: the Pillar, the Eternal Child, the Rebel, or the Invisible Child.

The Pillar, which is the most common adult child profile a clinician is likely to see, presents the following characteristics:

- Overly responsible
- Overachiever
- Perfectionist
- Dichotomous thinking
- Difficulty relaxing or being playful
- Controlling
- Rigid
- Articulate
- Neat and well groomed

- Compulsively organized
- Low self-esteem
- Self-worth based on what they do, not who they are
- Lack of fulfillment in virtually all areas of their lives
- No sense of boundaries
- Anticipate, and are more comfortable in, a crisis
- Extreme need for approval
- Extreme need to "fix" others
- Many somatic complaints

The Eternal Child will exhibit these characteristics:

- Very witty
- Low self-esteem
- Feelings of powerlessness
- Highly competitive
- Confusion
- Takes life so seriously that, in order to cope, appears to take nothing seriously
- Directionless
- Procrastination
- Dichotomous thinking
- Distracts self and others from problematic issues and feelings through humor or changing the subject
- Selects people (often impulsively) they perceive as perfect to utilize as a mentor, rescue them, fulfill all their needs
- Controlling
- Many somatic complaints
- Consistent disappointment in themselves or others
- Lack of clear interpersonal boundaries
- Choose critical or judgmental people as their significant other

The Rebel will generally display these characteristics:

- Behaviorally acts out feelings
- Possible alcohol or other drug abuse
- Impulsive
- Difficulty following through and completing tasks

- Angry
- Blaming
- Low self-esteem
- Underachiever
- Easily threatened
- Antagonistic
- Erratic behavior patterns
- Possessive and demanding in significant primary relationships
- Anticipates rejection and failure
- Controlling
- Assumes others feel and think as they do
- Lack of clear interpersonal boundaries
- Self-destructive behaviors
- Suicidal tendencies, ideation, or attempts

The Invisible Child will exhibit these characteristics:

- A strong fantasy life
- Socially isolated
- Overachievers
- Shy
- People-pleasers
- Rigid
- Detached from their feelings
- Look to others to define them
- Very fearful
- Phobic
- Distorted body image
- Low self-esteem
- Possible eating disorder
- Some somatic complaints
- Loneliness
- Feeling different or odd
- Define themselves by what they lack (versus assets)
- Extremely needy in relationships
- Difficulty letting go or separating
- Fearful of change

- Avoidance of confrontation at all cost
- A wish to be nonexistent, invisible, unnoticed
- Dichotomous thinking

DETERMINING IF A PATIENT IS AN ADULT CHILD

As early on in therapy as possible, it is critical that clinicians determine if a patient is indeed an adult child. Here is a suggested list of questions and a guideline as to the significance of the responses given.

Before a trusting relationship is developed with the therapist, the adult child may be in a lot of denial about past traumas and events. Therapists might not get full and complete answers at the onset of therapy, so it may be necessary to ask these questions throughout treatment.

1. *"Did either of your parents drink? If yes, how much and when?"*

A yes response requires further exploration because quantity is relative. One person's concept of a "normal" amount could be another person's concept of minimal or excessive. Alcoholism is not defined by the quantity of intake or the frequency of drinking, but by the compulsive need and compulsive regimentation of the drinking. An alcoholic can go to work sober and delay the need for a drink until 5:00 P.M., for example. Or an alcoholic may stay sober during the entire work week, drinking away the entire weekend. An alcoholic could drink all day, every day, or any variation of the above.

2. *"Did your grandparents drink?"*

A yes response requires the same exploration as in question number one. Compulsive and addictive personality traits, as well as rules regarding family structure and relationships, are commonly passed on from generation to generation without active addiction necessarily being present in each generation.

31

3. *"Were there any habits that any member of your family had to the extreme, such as working more than fifty hours a week, obesity or extreme thinness, legal or illegal drug use?"*

All addictions provide the same general profile and con-current results. The object of the compulsion (food, alcohol, Valium, cocaine, work, and so on) may vary, but the impact on the children and the family is relatively the same.

4. *"Is there any history of mental illness in your family?"*

Because alcoholism has been historically stigmatized, a family member may have been ostracized, abandoned, or "put away" with the label of "crazy" rather than identified as being an alcoholic. Frequently addiction to alcohol causes bizarre behavior. The family tends to label and focus on the manifes-tations — hence, interpreting the problem as mental illness — rather than identifying the source of the behavior: the disease of alcoholism.

5. *"Were you or anyone in your family sexually or physi-cally abused?"*

This is an important question to ask, though it may take establishment of trust within the therapeutic relationship to get an honest and complete answer. Often, if abuse of a person is occurring in a family, there is abuse of alcohol or other drugs, or both.

6. *"Who was most involved in caring for you physically and emotionally?"* *Have the patient describe how the caretaking occurred and was carried out.*

Emotional and physical neglect tend to be common experi-ences for adult children. Alcoholics are too self-involved and, when inebriated, too out of touch with reality to be available on a consistent basis for their children. Sober parents, when present, are too involved in their own survival and that of the alcoholic's to deal fully with the needs of their children.

7. *"Was there violence in your family of origin?"*

In alcoholic families, feelings and their expression are unacceptable. Usually, the only feeling consistently expressed is the alcoholic's anger. The family mobilizes around minimizing, avoiding, or preventing situations that could arouse the alcoholic's rage. Because the expression of feelings was so infrequent and emotional control was paramount, even yelling could be perceived as terrifying and violent. Because emotions were so repressed, anger could have been volcanic when finally let out and, as a result, violent in its delivery.

8. *"Are your biological parents still together? If not, what were the circumstances of their separation?"*

The answer to this question could provide a piece of loss history and clues as to how the family dealt with stress, pain, and relationships. It is also important to know if a parent committed suicide, as that child would be at greater risk to think of suicide as an option for him- or herself. The grief work, which is a necessary part of the healing process, would also be different for a person with a deceased parent.

9. *"How was physical affection expressed between yourself and your parents? Between your parents? Between you and your siblings? How was love expressed? How was anger expressed? How were disagreements handled?"*

These responses provide the beginning seeds of information about family rules, belief systems, roles, patterns of interaction, and styles of emotional communication. The clinician will probably find that real feelings were not directly expressed. Most frequently, the clinician will also hear that feelings were negatively labeled, such as disruptive, not nice, unimportant, or a sign of weakness. These basic ideas, learned within the family of origin, provide the foundation for either satisfying or dysfunctional relationships in adulthood.

10. *"Who, within your family of origin or outside of your family, were you able to confide in as a child? How old were you and what were the circumstances?"*

Explore if the adult child had any sources of support, nurturance, guidance, or refuge. More times than not, many of these children were emotionally isolated and had no safe place or person with whom they trusted to be themselves. In their times of perceived isolation, their feelings were more repressed and their lives were more stressful and chaotic.

11. *"Have any of your primary relationships been with an addict or alcoholic? Are you an addict or an alcoholic? What has your personal usage of alcohol or other drugs been like?"*

The clinician is looking for repetitive, dysfunctional patterns. Daughters of alcoholics are statistically more likely to choose an alcoholic as a partner. Sons of alcoholics are statistically more likely to become alcoholics themselves.[*] Additionally, the responses will help to indicate if the adult child has tried an alternative style of relationship, or if there continues to be an entrenchment in the dysfunctional, but familiar, patterns set by the family of origin.

If you assess that the person is an active alcoholic or other drug addict, the chemical dependency needs to be addressed first. The first steps in the healing process for an alcoholic or addict needs to be abstinence from mood-altering substances and working a recovery program. Once a person is in recovery for at least one year, he or she will be emotionally ready to deal with family-of-origin and adult child issues.

---

[*] Migs Woodside, "Children of Alcoholics," a Report to Hugh L. Carey, Governor of New York. Children of Alcoholics Foundation, July 1982.

CONCLUSION

During the initial assessment process of therapy, the clinician should get at least the following information in order to identify if the patient is an adult child of an alcoholic:

- The role or roles the patient played within his or her family of origin.
- How the patient sees the world and him- or herself.
- What coping skills have been learned.
- What intrapsychic defenses have been developed.

CHAPTER THREE

Stages of Healing — Characteristics, Tasks, And Interventions

This chapter provides a guide for the clinician to help adult children of alcoholics through the developmental stages of healing. Healing is defined as a whole life in which patients own and utilize their full personal power. Healing is self-forgiveness. It is the freedom to choose and to make responsible choices. It is a time of mourning and mending the hurt. It involves embracing the totality of who they are. It is seeing the pain, feeling the pain, then letting go, and moving on. The therapeutic healing process is progressive. It is also one of seemingly forward and backward movement. Progress in one healing stage may trigger an issue or developmental task of a previous stage. It is important for the clinician to know this and to explain this process to adult children.

These stages are to be used as a framework from which the therapist can organize his or her treatment plan. The interventions described are not necessarily exclusive to the stage in which they are denoted. They are suggestions to implement when adult children are confronting the particular struggles or issues indicative of that stage, but can be used in other stages of healing as well.

During each of the following stages, patients try on and practice new beliefs, responses, and behaviors. In session, choices are explored and processed. In daily life, new alternatives are rehearsed until ownership and integration occurs. Adult children experience cognitive dissonance regarding change and acting on their newfound choices. They may try out an option before they allow themselves to be a part of it. These are all steps toward establishing congruency between their behavior and their feelings.

The development of appropriate interpersonal boundaries is a thread throughout the therapeutic stages of healing. Adult children grapple with their sense of self — emotionally and physically. They seek to discover where they end and others begin, and strive to clearly differentiate between what they have control over and what they don't.

STAGE ONE — DISCOVERY

Characteristics and Symptomatology
Of the DISCOVERY Stage

When adult children of alcoholics are in the **DISCOVERY** stage of healing, they are experiencing the discomfort of an issue, or issues, that have been historically denied, repressed, or ignored. Their uneasiness with their present life, personhood, or relationships is the motivation that sets them on the path of therapeutic search and discovery. This may be at the onset of treatment or during the course of treatment, when a past trauma pushes itself into the adult child's conscious mind.

Adult children's defense structures shield them from the source of their disease. Their denial can manifest itself in many different ways. They may intellectualize their feelings or disconnect from the feelings associated with their origin of pain. If they have some recall of past traumas, they may minimize its impact: "It wasn't all that bad." Or they may minimize their own experience: "Others had it worse." Some may believe that their past difficulties did not affect them and have nothing to do with who they are today. For others, the situations that they were victim to were so unfathomable that they totally blocked them out, pretending not to know what they know, fearing they made them up, or perceiving the memories as only powerful, repetitive dreams.

Tasks to Accomplish
In the DISCOVERY Stage

The primary task for adult children to accomplish in the **DISCOVERY** stage is to get past the denial of their pain. As adult children begin to acknowledge the alcoholism in their family of origin, as they open their eyes to the traumas of their past, feelings start to surface, old beliefs don't fit, and basic coping skills don't seem to work as they once used to. Out of this confusion are born the seeds to question their lifestyles, challenge who they thought they were, and motivate a change. This discovery is very scary and often overwhelming. With this in mind, the therapist helps instill hope in the adult children that they can recover and assists them in developing the courage to proceed with the healing process.

Interventions to Implement
In the DISCOVERY Stage

The following are various techniques that the therapist can utilize to help patients accomplish the tasks of the **DISCOV-ERY** stage. They are subcategorized into detailed data gathering methods, educational tools, and experiential exercises.

Data Gathering Methods

The following is a process known as the *Emotional Life Line.* It is a structured way to gather vital history from adult children of alcoholics. It can reveal the possible themes, trends, stressors, parallels, and notable events in the adult child's life.

To begin, the therapist asks the patient to list all the names of significant family members, their relationships, religious affiliations, occupations, and their corresponding dates of birth. With each family member in mind, the adult child is asked to record the following events with their corresponding date (if applicable): death, divorce, mental illness, alcohol or other drug use, immigration, physical abuse, sexual abuse, and any other traumatic experience. The therapist verbally processes the information with the patient to obtain more details and connect feelings to the events described.

The therapist can also help the patient focus on a certain issue. The adult child selects a past event and expounds on it in either a prose format or by making a drawing. The content could be of the event itself, the adult child at the time of the event, or the important people involved in the event.

Educational Tools

Therapists assume several roles in their work with adult children of alcoholics. They need to be teachers as well as clinicians to be effective healers with this population. There is a dearth of information that adult children may lack. These range from basic social and life skills to more emotionally complex concepts that help them process their day-to-day experiences, rather than just reacting to them. In creating a formulation about themselves and life, they can then make some kind of positive, affirming sense of the world they live in, rather than being a victim to circumstance.

Over the course of treatment, information is provided to adult children to help them with each milestone they incur. Initially, the therapist **teaches about the disease of alcoholism.** Specifically discussed are the effects and impact of the disease on both the alcoholic and the alcoholic's entire family. There are numerous educational resources available in various mediums for the clinician to share with adult children of alcoholics, such as books, articles, films, and videotapes. A suggested reading list is included at the end of this book.

It is in this initial phase of therapy that the *therapist teaches about the healing process itself.* It is imperative to let adult children know that healing is a process; there is no instant solution or painless road to take. From each awareness comes growth, and consequently, more emotional freedom, increased self-worth, and a clearer awareness of the road yet to be traveled. With each change and with each step toward change, there is the possibility of an increase in the adult child's willingness to heal and to see he or she deserves to heal. By providing a progressive picture, the therapist can assuage some of the adult child's fears and expectations about the stages of healing.

Experiential Exercises

As the past comes into focus and is seen with greater understanding, feelings long hidden and repressed start to surface. The therapist helps adult children *name or label feelings, reinforce that they have permission to feel their feelings, and explore the advantages to experiencing feelings.* Usually as these shifts occur, adult children struggle with the new information and the resulting powerful emotions. A part of them may want to stay in denial, while another part is pulled toward fuller awareness. The therapist can help patients work through this struggle by *externalizing the conflict going on inside them.* By identifying, verbalizing, and then actually engaging in a discussion between the different factions within, adult children of alcoholics can

- increase interpersonal understanding.
- see the rewards and penalties to each part of their emotional tug-of-war.
- own and take responsibility for feelings, beliefs, and values connected to each side of the struggle. With responsibility comes the ability to make a conscious choice, rather than be a victim or a reactor to the denial.

The use of *storytelling and metaphors* is also helpful for the therapist to use in the **DISCOVERY** stage, as well as throughout the healing process. It is an indirect method of seeing, feeling, or experiencing that allows patients to transcend their conscious thought processes. New information is not threatening when offered this way; consequently, adult children don't need to use their denial to feel emotionally safe.

Therapeutic stories are defined as a complete tale with a beginning, middle, and an end. They communicate a direct, clear message to the listener. The body of the story is an obvious analogy to the patient's current dilemma, with the conclusion holding the salient point the therapist wishes to convey.

Metaphors are also stories, but they don't necessarily have a complete format and may be open-ended. They suggest an analogy and intimate a personal relatedness to the listener. Metaphors make indirect references using the listener's language and personal perspective. They offer therapeutic messages throughout, rather than placing the emphasis at the end.

The following is an example of a metaphor. It focuses on the movement out of denial and the attempt to trust enough to open up.

> *There once was a small boy who lived in a country far, far away. This boy was like other boys in all respects except one. He had an unusual habit. He wrote in books about all the important events that happened to him. He had done this ever since he had learned to write. As a result, he wrote of many, many things that occurred in his young life. These included moments of happiness, anguish, pain, insults, and hurt feelings. Perhaps even more unusual than his ability to quickly register the event in his books was the fact that once he wrote down the event and feeling, it went completely out of his memory. He didn't think about it or look back at it again.*
>
> *As years passed, he continued to grow up, and like other boys, wanted to achieve great things. Try as he*

might, however, he kept feeling compelled to go back to his books and record some new thing. As you might imagine, with every passing year, he accumulated a larger and larger volume of books filled with his writings. The books filled all kinds of different spaces in his room. Dust collected as the books formed their towers in this corner and that. They sat unmoved and loomed in large piles over the boy's head. Soon the books filled every corner and blocked the windows of his room. Events continued to happen in the boy's life, as events tend to do. He wrote in book after book. Eventually, he was only able to walk a narrow path in his room that he carefully carved from the cavernous wall of books around him.

Over the years, the boy was quite unhappy at times. He had no real understanding of why. He was never far from his precious load of books. They seemed to be all too much a part of what was natural to him. He was troubled by how he seemed so unaware of his past feelings and memories. Other boys talked about themselves and their past experiences.

As you might expect, news of this boy's unusual lifestyle spread. Living in a room full of books doesn't stay secret for long. Many people were curious about the boy, particularly an old, wise woman who lived nearby. She had watched him grow up. She had watched as he stopped to write in his books. The boy began to wonder what he could do with all his books. They were threatening to overrun his room and leave no space for him.

As he was wondering, he walked by the old woman. She asked him, "Why are you so lost in thought?"

The boy said, "I don't know what to do with all the books I have in my room. I no longer have room for me."

The sagely woman asked, "Do you read those books?"

The boy answered, "No, of course not. Why would I do that?"

The woman replied, "You have spent so many years collecting all those events and thoughts and feelings.

What use is all that life experience and information if it is frozen there inside your books? Bring those books out into the sunlight. Read them one by one. Let the thoughts, feelings, and events flow into your life here and now. All those books contain treasure to be used, treasure to be made a living part of your life."

The boy was stunned. He had never considered doing such a thing. The more he thought about it, the more curious he became. He wondered what really was in all those books and what it would be like to open them up. He felt a wave of fear come over him. He asked the woman, "If I begin to read the books, would you be able to be with me from time to time, to help me understand all that I am experiencing?"

"Yes, of course," the old woman said, and added, "Let's begin today."

Feelings never before given permission to surface, be experienced, or understood begin to seep into present-day consciousness during the **DISCOVERY** stage. In order to help patients cope with this change, the therapist can provide them *structured activities*. In doing so, adult children gain a sense of familiarity, control, and manageability over their emotions. One tool is the *Feelings Check List*. The therapist selects a list of at least ten feelings ranging from negative to positive. A suggested list is:

- Angry
- Sad
- Guilty
- Lonely
- Frustrated
- Ashamed
- Numb
- Insecure
- Joyful
- Cared for
- Confident
- Satisfied
- Loving
- Calm

The therapist can tailor this list to the specific needs and experiences of the individual with whom he or she is working. The patient marks on a chart or in a journal the following data to correspond with each feeling: the time of day the feeling occurred; a description of the circumstances or event that was going on; and who, if anyone, was also there.

STAGE TWO — SELF-BLAME

Characteristics and Symptomatology Of the SELF-BLAME Stage

In the **SELF-BLAME** stage, adult children generally have their memory intact. They carry the belief, however, that they are totally or to a great extent responsible for their past traumas. They try to gain control over their victimization by taking responsibility for it. They may express this directly: "I asked for it." "I must have set it up." "If only I had . . ." "If only I didn't . . ." This carries over into the here and now, asserting that they are the cause of any or most misunderstandings or misfortunes that befall them, acquaintances, or loved ones. They are usually filled with anger that they turn inward on themselves.

Tasks to Accomplish In the SELF-BLAME Stage

Though building self-esteem is a task the therapist works with all through the stages of healing, it is the critical focus of helping someone surpass **SELF-BLAME.** As children, many of these patients blamed themselves for the stress and strife around them. They saw stress as a just punishment or as a condition perpetuated by them. The impact of this personalization is a negative self-image. They may maintain this image by continuing to assign themselves hostile and catastrophic powers. Even the anger felt toward others is turned inward and used as yet another way to nullify themselves.

Rather than blaming their abusers or people who hurt them, they blame themselves with comments such as, "What did I do to make him react like that?"

To initiate breaking this pattern, the therapist introduces the concept of interpersonal boundaries. It is in this stage that patients begin to grasp the ideas of separateness, individuation, and differentiation.

Adult children of alcoholics need to establish a balance of responsibility, as opposed to blaming themselves for everything. In this stage, they are encouraged to take responsibility for themselves in a positive, loving, affirming way. They start to develop beliefs that work in their favor. The focus shifts from just trying to survive to seeking ways in which to thrive. They discover and build on their strengths and, as a result, learn to increase trust in themselves. They begin to give themselves permission to make mistakes without drawing the conclusion that they are total failures. Conversely, they take their first steps toward reevaluating their drive to be perfect, which is motivated by fear.

This negative self-image also impacts their relationships with others. They don't feel worthy of receiving love. They don't feel they are lovable for who they are, only for what they do. Consequently, another task of this stage is to learn that there are other ways to feel loved and to give love than by fostering dependency. They learn about the various forms of love and explore the different kinds of satisfying relationships they can create and be a part of.

During this stage, much examination of the family of origin occurs. The recognition of childhood traumas and identification of the consequent needs that went unfulfilled are in themselves healing tasks. Therapists can use this knowledge to help make conscious connections for the patients between what they lived through, the belief systems they developed in order to understand and cope with their world, and the feelings and behavior that they manifest today.

Interventions to Implement
In the SELF-BLAME Stage

The following are various techniques that the therapist can utilize to help adult children accomplish the tasks of the **SELF-BLAME** stage. They are subcategorized into detailed data gathering methods, educational tools, and experiential exercises.

Data Gathering Methods

Throughout the healing process, the therapist helps the patient **bring into conscious awareness the past and how it has effected the present.** In the **SELF-BLAME** stage, the therapist conducts a vigilant inquiry of significant childhood traumas. With the investigative ability of a skilled detective, the therapist assists the adult child in accessing the most complete memories, including the most subtle emotional nuances, the most minute perceptions. The data gathering should include not just details of each event, but also identification of the resultant unfulfilled needs, the consequent coping behaviors that were developed, and the beliefs that were perpetuated in order to rationalize and understand the trauma.

Educational Tools

During the **SELF-BLAME** stage, patients can be far removed from their self-worth. The therapist can help them become aware of their personal value by *telling them their strengths* along with how and where these attributes are being successfully applied. Often their self-worth is further denigrated by responses, both emotional and behavioral, that work against their best interest. These reactions are almost instinctive, coming from a place of learned habit or ritual. The therapist *challenges these old thought patterns by pointing out their repetitive nature and their negative consequences.* The therapist expands the adult child's awareness by *illustrating the choices* available to that person. It is stressed that everyone has choices in every situation. The therapist can utilize this technique within the full spectrum of decision making — from basic to more complex.

Some adult children are so stuck in catastrophic, omnipotent thinking and so full of self-blame for all the negative events in their lives that they are totally blind to the concept of choice. Adult children have choices in how they respond to others and to the circumstances in their lives, just as the people around them have choices in how they respond. This may seem simplistic, but this awareness is a vital first step for adult children in establishing boundaries and balance in their relationships.

Another consequence to poor self-image is disproportionate relationships in regard to need satisfaction and emotional fulfillment. Frequently, adult children will sacrifice themselves by negating or minimizing their feelings and desires in order to sustain their relationships. The global payoff to this sacrificial behavior is the hope that the significant other will desperately need and therefore stay in the patient's life. *The therapist and the patient look into the rewards of being depended on and totally responsible for the continuance of the relationship.* Together, they take a microscopic view of how this may be occurring in the adult child's relationships. Once the therapist and adult child identify these relationships, they investigate the emotional ramifications of the adult child being the sole carrier of the relationship. The most common conclusions that are derived are feelings of invisibility, nonexistence, exhaustion, and depletion.

At this point in the healing process, the therapist *questions and confronts the patient's belief system about his or her own needs.* For example, "If others have needs, isn't it possible you do too?" *The adult child learns of his or her needs by identifying and labeling the needs of others.* Because they are perceptive and sensitive to others, adult children are very tuned-in to what may satisfy or make someone else happy. The therapist helps patients use their already well-honed abilities in order to circuitously learn about themselves.

Experiential Exercises

Adult children tend to carry into their adulthood the beliefs and perceptions they learned as children. As adults, they still contend that it is not permissible to acknowledge or trust their feelings. When recalling memories, adult children most frequently describe their childhoods in an objective, narrative tone, as if telling someone else's story. *The therapist makes use of this emotional distancing defense by labeling the person in the memory as* **the child,** *and the person who is recalling the memory,* **the adult.** The therapist then asks the adult to use his or her wisdom in assessing the child's experience.

It is necessary for the adult child of an alcoholic to teach his or her child within not to deny needs, fears, insecurities, or instincts, nor to punish him- or herself for having them. The therapist assists the adult child in connecting to and nurturing his or her child within by affirming the totality of his or her past experiences. This can be done by the therapist asking the adult child detailed questions about the memory, such as:

- "What responsibility did the child really have?"
- "Did the child have the power it ascribed him- or herself?"
- "Was the child the cause of the event or the victim?"
- "What was the child feeling when this event was taking place?"
- "What did the child need?"
- "What conclusions did the child draw about him- or herself? About relationships? About life? About his or her role?"
- "Does the adult agree with all of these perceptions?"
- "Could there be other ways to look at what happened?"

In focusing on the memory in detail, along with questioning and confronting the deductions made, patients begin to see themselves in a new light. The burden of self-blame begins to lift, and in its place, the seeds of creating positive, self-affirming beliefs about themselves are planted.

Adult children of alcoholics tend to emotionally distance themselves or totally shut down with hopes of protecting themselves from the world and the people in it, as well as to protect others from themselves. Rather than taking the risk of exhibiting their true personhood and feelings, they may portray a persona they believe will satisfy the needs of the persons or situations at hand. The more they playact, the more removed they become from themselves. The further they get from themselves, the more indistinct and impalpable become their own feelings, thoughts, needs, opinions, and values. It is a method of coping they learned as children and continue to use as adults.

The therapist can challenge the use of different personas, and thereby open the doors to choice for patients. One way is the use of *Creative Mask Making* in the therapeutic session. Patients are instructed to draw and create a mask to represent each persona they present to the world. The patient places one of the masks in front of his or her face. The experience is explored as the therapist leads the adult child into increased insight:

- "If the mask could talk, what would it say?"
- "What does the mask protect you from?"
- "What does the mask protect others from?"
- "What is behind the mask?"
- "How does it feel to be behind the mask?"

Also discussed, are the consequences to wearing a mask:

- It blocks intimacy.
- It blocks genuine, honest contact.
- It takes enormous amounts of psychic energy to hide behind and maintain the mask.
- It causes the repression, denial, and inhibition of feelings.
- It inhibits change by obstructing emotional and developmental movement.

It is appropriate at the **SELF-BLAME** stage of healing to encourage patients to reach out for *support and emotional contact*. One option is attendance at ACOA or Al-Anon meetings (please refer to Chapter Four, Adjunctive Therapies in a Group Format, for a description of the nature and purpose of these self-help support groups). It is not unusual for adult children to be socially isolated. Embolden them to make at least one or two social contacts a week outside of their job setting. They may need to start with phone calls and work up to face-to-face social activities. Also, the acquisition of a pet may be suggested. Frequently, a pet increases the owner's self-esteem by making it possible to receive unconditional, positive regard. With a pet, therefore, the adult child can safely risk emotional bonding without fear of rejection. The nature of a relationship with a pet also assists the patient in learning how to be responsible for a person in a new way.

STAGE THREE — VYING FOR CONTROL

Characteristics and Symptomatology
Of the VYING FOR CONTROL Stage

In this stage of the healing process, patients are shifting the blame for the pain in their lives from themselves to outside themselves. They are in touch with their anger, but it is nonspecifically directed. The anger is diffused, generalized, and pervasive. They tend to engage in a great deal of judgmental "finger pointing" at others. In the **SELF-BLAME** stage, they feel totally responsible for everything, but in this stage, they feel they are victims to the things and people in their lives. They feel filled with self-pity and a sense of powerlessness over themselves, their world, and others. They tend to feel overwhelmed and immobilized by the magnitude of their memories and emotions. As a result, they may procrastinate, avoid making decisions, and give both direct and indirect messages to not expect much, if anything, from themselves.

A cautious note to therapists: This is a very delicate time for adult children. Their rage and fear may be so intense that they may choose to regress, drop out of therapy, become extremely depressed, or act out. Because of their propensity for dichotomous thinking, patients at this stage may lose touch with any progress they have made, any positive memories they might have accessed, and appear very pessimistic about their present and their future. The therapist needs to anticipate the adult child's resistance to further therapeutic growth and work with it and through it. Many adult children get stuck in this stage and never get past feeling like a victim.

Adult children will, in general, represent themselves in the **VYING FOR CONTROL** stage in one of three manners. We choose to label them as the Complainer, the Glutton, and the Aggressor.

The Complainer will overtly act as very much the victim. There is an abundance of self-pity and a relentless seeking of attention through moaning, groaning, and obvious acts of martyrdom. Life is seen through the Complainer's eyes as something bad, as something one endures.

The Glutton appears consumed with their own needs and personhood. They have a very narrow focus and see the world as revolving around and reflecting off of them. They feel easily deprived and seek immediate gratification. Most frequently, Gluttons are compulsive overeaters. They tend to reduce stress or pursue emotional solace through food.

The Aggressor's predominant visage is one of anger. They are easily frustrated and feel easily threatened. They have extremely short fuses and are seen as overreactive to incidences others would perceive as minor. In being highly reactive, they are disposed to throwing tantrums in an attempt to gain control.

**Tasks to Accomplish
In the VYING FOR CONTROL Stage**

As in the **SELF-BLAME** stage, patients' self-perception plays a major role in their perceptions of the world and in their healing process. In the **VYING FOR CONTROL** stage, the therapist again focuses on developing self-esteem. Patients learn how to make time for themselves, not just for everyone else. They learn how to give to themselves and take care of themselves, versus depending on and waiting for others to do it for them. They begin, in small increments, to internalize and own the good feelings and positive feedback given them by others, as well as allow joyful experiences to be a safe part of their lives. They start building trust in themselves, and as they do, they progressively risk showing and sharing their real feelings and opinions.

Cognitively, they formulate the concept of choice as an alternative to responding out of old programmed habits and beliefs. They acquire the ability to gain control over situations, rather than being immobilized by their fears. They develop effective problem-solving methods. They learn to concretely and specifically identify how they behaviorally and emotionally express their fears and anxieties. These skills gradually take the place of persistent and compulsive worrying. Additionally, they begin to discover the "gray." They expand their awareness beyond the black-and-white, all-or-nothing approach they have traditionally brought to ideas, thoughts, feelings, relationships, and goals.

Family-of-origin issues continue to be explored. In the **VYING FOR CONTROL** stage, patients finally grieve and mourn the numerous losses experienced in their lives due to parental alcoholism. These include but are not limited to the losses of childhood, nurturance, safety, innocence, and security. They let go of the fantasy of what they hoped for and therefore brought themselves to believe about their family and childhood. They see the reality and feel its impact. The results are painful, but healing. Reality facilitates more balance in their lives, particularly within the personal realm of relationships. The enmeshment with the family of origin begins to break and in its place is the establishment of interpersonal boundaries.

Interventions to Implement
In the VYING FOR CONTROL Stage

The following are various techniques that the therapist can utilize to help adult children accomplish the tasks of the **VYING FOR CONTROL** stage. They are subcategorized into detailed data gathering methods, educational tools, and experiential exercises.

Data Gathering Methods

In this stage, the therapist must gather more information about the adult child's past. The purpose of acquiring more history information in the **VYING FOR CONTROL** stage is to activate the grieving process. The therapist asks the patient to *record every loss* that he or she can remember. The patient is to include the date each loss occurred; what feelings he or she had at the time, if any; the circumstances of the loss; and the people involved in the memory. Identifying their loss experiences also allows adult children to label, track, and own the skills and tools they developed in order to cope with their losses. These may include becoming:

- extremely competent
- a leader
- an overachiever
- independent
- self-sufficient
- rich with imagination

Educational Tools

In the **VYING FOR CONTROL** stage, the therapist facilitates further internalization of positive self-worth. The therapist continues to *directly affirm and validate the patient's personhood, independent thinking, thoughts, feelings, and opinions* Additionally, the therapist *teaches self-nurturance exercises that work toward overall wellness.* These may include encouragement of a healthy diet and the benefits of physical exercise. The therapist *teaches the value of positive affirmations to increase self-esteem,* for instance, to tell oneself consciously, *I deserve it.... I count.... I'm important.... I'm lovable.* The therapist also discusses with the patient the importance of making time for and implementing on a regular basis activities that pamper him- or herself. They brainstorm concrete ways the patient can bring lightness, joy, and play into his or her life.

In session, patients are instructed on and practice the use of relaxation techniques. There are numerous creative methods of relaxation the therapist can draw from. The following are a few examples:

- guided imagery
- full-body, progressive relaxation
- focused, regulated breathing
- prayer
- meditation

In the **VYING FOR CONTROL** stage of healing, patients become receptive to learning alternatives to self-defeating thought processes. *The therapist provides them with a framework to use in making decisions and solving problems.* We suggest a clear, step-by-step model.

1. Identify and define exactly what the dilemma is. Adult children tend to get overwhelmed by their feelings and lose sight of the core issue.
2. Explore every possible option — rational and irrational. Adult children may be used to limiting themselves by what they believe others expect of them and by old, dysfunctional belief systems.
3. Assess the consequences of each option. Assist them in asking themselves which option they could live with or which option comes closest to meeting their needs. These patients may need much assistance with this step as they are, generally, far removed from knowing their own needs.

4. After weighing the various options, make a choice and take action. Many adult children will require a lot of support to take this step. Reinforce to them that they are separate from their decisions. They may realize later that their decision was not optimal, but that doesn't mean that they are wrong or bad. Teach them that virtually no decision is permanent, that they can always make a new decision. Also, let them know there are no mistakes, no successes, no failures, only experiences from which to learn and grow.

Many adult children experience a persistent feeling of dread, which is exacerbated by circular, persistent worrying. These patients benefit from learning alternatives to being immobilized by their fears. Initially, they must learn to *own their fears*, rather than deny them, perseverate on them, or punish themselves for having them. Once they're able to own and accept their fears, they can then diminish them, control them, or eliminate them through action.

Upon verbalizing their worries and acknowledging their underlying fears, *encourage these patients to talk their concerns through to the end of their projected story. Discuss and explore the possible worst-case scenarios. Assist them in creating at least two choices of action if their worst fears are realized. Help them see, in reality, what they have control over and what they don't.* This approach validates their feelings and gives them direction and effective control.

During the **VYING FOR CONTROL** stage, patients tend to experiment with and try on many new interactional behaviors. The feelings that ensue, and the new and different responses others may have to the adult child's changes, can result in resistance to further change, relapse, or regression. This may be averted by the *therapist predicting to adult children the various possible consequences to their internal changes.* This helps them gain control over their situations, rather than being immobilized by their fears. It also facilitates them seeing the bigger picture and increases their awareness of the impact they have on others and the world around them. The predictions are concretely discussed and detailed.

In the area of primary relationships, prepare the patient for his or her significant others' anticipated reactions. Partners and family members tend to escalate their dysfunctional behavior in order to maintain the status quo. Exaggerate the various possible scenarios to best prepare the patient for what may happen.

In this stage, adult children are likely to feel a major shift in their perceptions of themselves. *Encourage them to internalize positive feelings and experiences in small increments.* "Good" feelings can be awkward and unfamiliar to adult children. Their discomfort with what they are unsure of, combined with their guilt for having "good" feelings, may be overwhelming. If not predicted and if not absorbed in small doses, positive feelings can result in self-recrimination, discounting, and possible relapse.

In all the healing stages, and particularly in the **VYING FOR CONTROL** stage, these patients will reach an impasse, exhibit resistance, or unconsciously want to slow down their healing process. One way this may be illustrated is the repeated focus on present-day problems or day-to-day crises. If the therapist abets the adult child by limiting the therapeutic work to putting out current fires, only superficial change will occur. Instead, *assist the patient in relating both the perceptions and the handling of present situations to the learnings of a child in an alcoholic family.* Once the connections are made, the therapist aids him or her in developing new skills and choices.

Experiential Exercises

The **VYING FOR CONTROL** stage is an opportunity for therapists to really stretch their creativity in the interventions they use. We suggest the following, but as with all the stages, these are just the seedlings for the therapist's imagination.

Have adult children write letters, with no intent to mail them. This is an effective tool to get closure on an event, relationship, or feeling. They can write a letter to someone to describe their needs or purge their emotions. They can write a letter to themselves from a significant other asking for forgiveness. To further intensify this experience, they can read the letter aloud in the therapy session. If they write the letter to purge themselves of anger toward a person, this may help them transcend the anger and bring forth a previously hidden dimension of understanding and compassion. When the rage is momentarily lifted, other feelings such as pain, hurt, and disappointment are released. Feelings long repressed and denied are expressed, accepted, validated, and set free. The adult child's defenses are temporarily down, and out of his or her vulnerability comes healing.

Encourage adult children to keep a journal or diary. This daily ritual has several benefits. It provides a time for patients to slow down and reflect on themselves, their feelings, and their day's events. It helps them sort out and organize their thoughts and emotions. The writing is an outlet for feelings that were historically pushed aside, rationalized away, ignored, or neglected. Also, it acts as a way to step outside themselves, to gain objectivity, to see a problem or issue from another perspective.

Instruct adult children in making a therapeutic collage. Utilizing magazines, glue, cardboard, and scissors, patients can cut up magazines to create a picture on cardboard depicting their family of origin, their fantasy image of their family of origin, the present family they have created, and themselves. This brings into conscious awareness the adult child's images and conceptualizations of the collage topic. Patients can then discuss and explore feelings and beliefs about the topic, the collage, and the psychological material that doing the collage provoked to the surface.

Concretely assist adult children in making the shift from habitual responses to seeing options and choices. The therapist aids patients in tracking and identifying rigid behavioral patterns they learned within their family of origin. Patients recall the origin of a specific belief in detail: who taught it to them, under what circumstances was it learned, how was it reinforced. Adult children are asked to re-create that past experience in the present, looking at how it was effective for them as children. The patient then explores if the childhood response fits with his or her life now, as an adult. Then the different options open to the adult child are discussed now that he or she is an adult. It is reinforced to the patient that he or she can still respond with behaviors that are old and familiar. With awareness, old behaviors are a choice adult children can make consciously and for which they have responsibility. It is their choice to act out of what used to be habit, and it is also their choice to select new alternative responses or solutions.

For many adult children, their parents' words, messages, and images are carried with them and appear as an ever-present obstacle in their significant relationships. These adult children may respond to other people as if they were their parent. They see and hear their parent instead of the person with whom they are relating. Under these circumstances, patients may seek approval — at all cost — from the person with whom they are relating. They are looking to get the needs met that weren't met by their parents. *The therapist helps the adult child identify and work with the rejecting and disapproving parents within the adult child.*

In separating out the parent, the adult child is freer to delineate between what is real and what isn't, between which expectations are realistic and which aren't. It also frees the adult child from a compulsive drive to receive unconditional love, and from the perpetual self-recriminations and self-blame for not getting his or her parents' unconditional love. Additionally, it opens the doors to conscious choice in relationships and responses, rather than reacting out of habit.

Assist adult children who have a disapproving internal parent to take responsibility for continually asking for the love they want from those who don't give it. The therapist helps the patient investigate the payoffs of asking directly and indirectly for love, only to not receive it. Adult children have an option to live with their frustration; again, let them experience choice. These patients are not responsible if people in their lives are not receptive to their clearly stated needs. They are responsible, however, for what they need and for who they choose to keep in their lives.

Adult children have difficulty setting and maintaining boundaries between themselves and others. It is critical for them to be able to establish differentiation behaviorally, emotionally, and physically. *To increase awareness, concretely walk through an incident in which blurred boundaries were a factor.* The therapist can help re-create the dialogue between the adult child and the person involved in a particular incident. Have the patient express his or her feelings, views, behaviors in the given situation. The therapist recants and separates for the adult child as he or she speaks: "That is your partner's feelings. Give only your opinion; your partner will have a chance in a minute." Then, the adult child physically moves into another chair and plays the role of the other person, expressing that person's behaviors and perceptions. The therapist continues to show the points of separation. The therapist underlines individual responsibility for choices made, feelings felt, and actions taken.

This intervention is also effective if the therapist is involved in the role-play. The therapist can act as the person engaging in dialogue with the adult child. The adult child and the therapist then switch: the adult child acting as the other person, and the therapist playing the role of the adult child. The interaction is then processed afterward.

Adult children of alcoholics need to grieve the numerous emotional and spiritual losses they have had in their lives. They need to say good-bye to the pain of the past and the power it has had over their lives. They must mourn their childhood and the trauma it represents. The therapist helps them to grieve their lost innocence, their fantasies of what their family was like, and the unfulfilled hopes for something more. The adult child identifies specific areas of deprivation: what they were cheated out of and from whom, and what they did not receive and from whom.

As the adult child goes through the grieving process, there will probably be resistance to letting go of the pain. The pain is familiar. The traumas have been leading them around and controlling their lives. They have virtually built their lives in response to their hurts and fears. *Help the adult child be tender and compassionate in putting the pain aside, and then letting it go.*

By grieving the past, adult children can cease hopelessly hoping. They free themselves from the shackles of the fantasy or ideal image of their parents and childhood. They begin to accept the reality of what was. Through awareness, they gain control. They acquire the ability to separate their present selves from the once firm grasp of their past. They take a major step away from feeling like a victim and, along with it, from the feelings of powerlessness and generalized, externalized anger and blame.

It is important to reinforce to adult children that in grieving their past traumas, they don't have to also deny the good. Adult children tend toward polarization in their perceptions. They can release the pain and the power it has had over them and still keep and cherish the good aspects of their childhood, their parents, and their family of origin.

When adult children relive the pain, the traumas, and the losses, it reinforces for them the high cost of depending on others. Emotional closeness has been equated with abandonment, rejection, and disappointment. As a result of their past experiences, they most frequently isolate or distance themselves from others emotionally. The therapist can help patients separate their past from the present by having them make up a *Present Resource List.* The list is comprised of people who are emotionally available to them. The patients break down ways in which each person on the list can realistically be there for them. It is stressed that no one person can fulfill their needs. This task gives adult children some control in relationships. They are not helpless as to what they get and from whom they get it.

STAGE FOUR — RIGHTEOUS ANGER

Characteristics and Symptomatology
Of the RIGHTEOUS ANGER Stage

In the **RIGHTEOUS ANGER** stage of healing, adult children begin to feel empowered. The anger, which was general and pervasive in the **VYING FOR CONTROL** stage, is now focused on the person or persons who hurt them. Their anger feels justified, and the source is known. Frequently, adult children in this stage have fantasies and strong desires to seek punishment or revenge for the perceived injustices done to them. They have strong feelings of indignation, and they promise themselves that they will never be victims to anyone or anything again.

Tasks to Accomplish
In the RIGHTEOUS ANGER Stage

The primary focus of the **RIGHTEOUS ANGER** stage is the adult child's emotional experiences. They learn to identify and live through the feelings from childhood and adolescence that they have long kept hidden from themselves. In feeling what was, they further differentiate between what is a habitual response from the past, and what is a response to the circumstances of the present. They allow themselves to intrinsically feel, own, and let go of some of their anger. In getting by the barrier of anger, they are freer to release on emotional, physical, and spiritual levels their other repressed and blocked emotions. As a result, they are more open to learning to practice and gain comfort in new ways of feeling and being. Finally, the ultimate goal of the **RIGHTEOUS ANGER** stage is to escape the bondage of self-blame and forgive themselves.

Interventions to Implement
In the RIGHTEOUS ANGER Stage

The following are various techniques the therapist can utilize to help adult children accomplish the tasks of the

RIGHTEOUS ANGER stage. If the patient has been in ongoing therapy with the same therapist, further specific informational disclosure would probably not be pertinent in this and further stages of the healing process. Therefore, the interventions are subcategorized to only educational tools and experiential exercises.

Educational Tools

The therapist iterates for the patient the unsophistication and powerlessness of children in an alcoholic family. The therapist reminds the adult child that the coping skills developed, the beliefs and values internalized, and the decisions made were all out of a strong sense of survival. Today, as adults, they have wisdom, choice, and power. These truths help counteract the self-blame and self-recrimination for perceived victimization, mistakes, and lost time.

The **RIGHTEOUS ANGER** stage is a time of self-discovery and trying on new behaviors. *Consistently bolster and encourage the adult child's implementation of new beliefs and choices.* Each new response is a risk and requires courage from the patient. Reinforce that there are no wrong moves, only lessons about life, others, and themselves to be learned.

Experiential Exercises

To broaden adult children's panorama of emotions, they can devise several kinds of Feelings Lists. One is a list of feelings from the most to least expressed as experienced in childhood and adolescence. With the therapist, the patient explores the sources of the feelings, as well as discusses and explores the emotionally-laden information that surfaces as a result.

Another list, from most to least, is of emotions felt in the present that go unexpressed. The precursors to these feelings are discussed. This list is explored and compared to the previous list, looking at what impeded expression then, and what impedes it now.

Another list can be made, again from most to least, of feelings both felt and expressed in childhood and adolescence.

It is processed as were the first two lists. And a final list can be made, from most to least, of feelings expressed in the present. It is discussed, as were the first three lists, with additional investigation as to what rules and reinforcers have been and are operating that give or don't give permission for feelings to be asserted.

Adult children can harbor a great deal of anger. It is vital to the healing process that they release it. The following are suggested means to this therapeutic end. Please note that these are only a few of the ways to assist adult children with their anger.

Use Bataka Bats in the therapeutic session. Bataka Bats are thickly padded, foam rubber bats with plastic handles. They are approximately the same size as a baseball bat, but much lighter in weight. We suggest patients hit the Bataka Bat against a chair, sofa, or pillow. We strongly recommend that the bat not be used on the therapist or another person, as this can scare adult children and confuse them as to the direction of their anger.

Instruct the adult children to bend their knees while in action so they don't injure their back. Every time the patients hit with the bat, have them verbalize their angry feelings toward a specific person. They can either say sentences such as, "I hate you!" or, "I resent you!" or they can make potent, emotional sounds. They may initially feel self-conscious and at a loss where to begin this exercise. The therapist can alleviate some of this anxiety by acting as a coach. Stand next to the patient as he or she uses the bat and say the words or noises with the patient. At first this may be in a slow, soft voice. The adult child is led in the releasing process by the therapist as he or she raises the tone and volume of his or her voice.

Most frequently, the angry feelings that begin their expression through yelling, screaming, or grunting change into sadness and tears. When this happens, allow the release process to go with this emotional shift and support the patient as he or she releases the pain. As a postscript, the same exercise can be done without Bataka Bats. Adult children can use their hands directly to hit a well-padded surface.

Direct the adult child in role-play. First ask the patient to identify a person and situation that makes him or her angry. The adult child acts as him- or herself. The person to whom the anger is directed can be an empty chair, a doll positioned in the chair, or a role taken on by the therapist. The patient verbalizes the anger toward the person. The therapist assists by emotionally priming the patient to get closer and deeper into his or her anger.

Patients can write letters to the persons with whom they are angry. These letters are not written with the intent to mail. It is a safe method to purge pent-up anger, frustration, and resentment. After a letter is written, it furthers the emotional liberation for the letter to be shredded or burned.

On separate pieces of paper, the adult child writes down the names of the people with whom he or she feels unresolved anger. The pieces of paper are then strewn on a couch or cushion. The patient is instructed and encouraged to hit the cushion, focusing on and letting out the anger felt toward the people whose names are on the papers.

The therapist can utilize verbal or physical assertion exercises. This is begun with the patient standing up. Patients bend their arms at the elbow and then thrust their arms straight back. This is labeled *action A*. The patients then thrust their arms forward, as if pushing something away. This is labeled *action B*. With each action a corollary verbalization is made. The following are examples of what patients could say with each action:

A — "Get off my back!"   B — "Get out of my life!"
A — "I'm tired of you!"   B — "Get away from me!"
A — "Stop it!"   B — "Go Away!"
A — "Not anymore!"   B — "Leave me alone!"

The action, done with the words, is repeated over and over with the therapist soliciting greater intensity and volume from the patient.

Encourage patients to carry out a physical exercise routine. Discuss the numerous activities available to them that would be enjoyable and rewarding. Exercise can relieve stress, increase one's energy level, give one a sense of accomplishment, increase self-worth, and act as a psychic release of pent-up feelings. Before beginning an exercise program, ensure that patients consult their physician so they don't begin a program that could be hazardous.

STAGE FIVE — IDENTITY AND BOUNDARIES

Characteristics and Symptomatology
Of the IDENTITY AND BOUNDARIES Stage

By the **IDENTITY AND BOUNDARIES** stage of healing, adult children begin moving toward taking real ownership of their lives. They have reclaimed their personal power. Habitual responses are at a minimum, if at all. They are recognizing and acting on the choices available to them. They are no longer in denial of their past or their feelings. Neither are they wallowing in their experience. There is a strong sense of and appreciation for the fact that they are survivors. They have freed themselves from the prison of self-blame. They have achieved self-forgiveness and intrinsically know they have done the best they could. Concurrently, they no longer feel only anger for the people who have hurt or harmed them. They can claim some understanding and see beyond the abusiveness to other attributes in the people who have harmed them. All of their energy is not solely tied up in their own existence and in trying to keep their heads above water. They are ready and willing to give to and help others. Lastly, they have developed a sense of humor. They have the ability to feel and express joy. They can embrace life with all its perfection, imperfection, and absurdities.

Tasks to Accomplish
In the IDENTITY AND BOUNDARIES Stage

Patients in the **IDENTITY AND BOUNDARIES** stage are bringing balance into their lives — within themselves, their reationships, in how they view their past, and in how they live in the present. Within themselves, they continue to process and work through unresolved feelings. They are allowing themselves greater self-appreciation. They are becoming more inner-directed and more trusting of their own instincts, feelings, and perceptions. As a result, they decrease their dependence on therapy, the therapist, friends, family, and loved ones for guidance. They are nearing a clearer sense of self-worth. This is evidenced by the establishment of a comfortable independence and an esteem for their individuality. They willingly take responsibility for themselves, their actions, and the consequences of their actions.

In relationships, adult children in this stage are testing and reinforcing their interpersonal boundaries. It is permissible to say no, to mean it, and to follow through with it. They are developing realistic expectations of themselves and others. They learn that their needs are righteous, that they are entitled to those needs. They recognize that their needs are valid, even if no one at a given moment can meet them.

Patients in this stage are also reconciling their past. Having thrown off some of their anger and bitterness, they begin to identify both strengths and weaknesses in their parents. They are open to acknowledgment of positive memories, good times, and likable attributes of their family of origin and individual family members. They also give recognition to the people who were there for them, who helped pull them through the difficult periods of their lives. They allow themselves to feel gratitude for those who offered and gave them the emotional sustenance that helped them to survive.

At this point, adult children of alcoholics are at last ready to enjoy and celebrate. The once constant feelings of dread, fear, and anxiety are gone or are quickly alleviated. They learn to relax and integrate concrete stress reduction techniques into their routines. Concurrently, they are more comfortable with playing and having fun. This gives rise to the vivacity and merriment of their long-hidden inner child.

Interventions to Implement
In the IDENTITY AND BOUNDARIES Stage

The following are various techniques that the therapist can utilize to help adult children accomplish the tasks of the **IDENTITY AND BOUNDARIES** stage. Generally, therapy by this stage of the healing process is more *directed and paced by the adult child,* rather than structured and led by the therapist. Patients benefit from being given full permission to trust themselves and take risks. The more control they are given in the therapy session, the more this is made possible. *Encourage them to utilize their own tools and abilities to come to their own conclusions,* versus providing for them the tools or the possible options in a given situation. Also, model life as balanced within the therapy session. Life is not always problem-focused, serious, and in need of scrutiny. *Incorporate humor, fun activities, and play into the therapy sessions.* These will aid in diffusing and de-intensifying events and feelings. They will also help patients laugh at themselves and give free vent to their child within.

As in the **RIGHTEOUS ANGER** stage, the interventions are subcategorized into educational tools and experiential exercises.

Educational Tools

Much of the **IDENTITY AND BOUNDARIES** stage deals with adult children affirming and implementing their newly discovered tools and skills, as well as establishing symmetry in their lives. To assist them in achieving this end, the therapist can use *metaphors, stories, and self-referential anecdotes (real or fictional).* For adult children, this will:

- reinforce their normalcy.
- describe options open to them.
- affirm their feelings.
- explain or validate appropriate interpersonal boundaries.

Healing, at this point, feels more positive and gratifying, yet patients still need to be motivated and emboldened with the courage to take the risky steps of independence and change. Therefore, *continue to reinforce their strengths, internal resources, and ability not to just survive, but to thrive.* Help them slow down in order to gain focus, to experience and appreciate themselves and the moment. This can be done by learning *relaxation techniques.* A few examples are:

- pausing and slowly counting to ten
- deep breathing
- inhaling for four counts, holding for eight counts, exhaling for four counts
- full-body, progressive relaxation exercises
- reading positive affirmations aloud or silently

Experiential Exercises

In order to help adult children concretely apply what they have learned within the therapeutic sessions to their daily lives, *the therapist can regularly assign tasks to do outside of the therapy session.* The patient utilizes these tasks as a method of focusing on and practicing a new skill, response, belief, or behavior. The therapist frames the task as an educational experience about the self — there is no success or failure in how it is executed. The task is then reviewed in the subsequent session. Discussed are the insights gained and any obstacles that arose during its completion.

The following is a suggested list of tasks that the therapist can encourage adult children, in the **IDENTITY AND BOUNDARIES** stage of the healing process, to do outside the therapy session.

1. *Help patients do activities for themselves, rather than doing them to satisfy someone else.*

Have them practice self-care: pamper and indulge themselves, play sports, get their hair cut, go shopping. With each activity, they say to themselves, *This is for me.*

2. **Have adult children make up a Self-Appreciation List.**

This is a list of what an adult child does for him- or herself and what he or she does for others.

3. **Have patients practice letting go of control.**

For example, at a family gathering, the adult child may always be the organizer. He or she can step back from this role. The adult child experiences not taking over, not taking care of everyone else. Predict to the patients their probable awkwardness and discomfort with this task.

4. **Have patients give themselves verbal affirmations.**

On a daily basis, they look at themselves in the mirror and verbalize positive statements about themselves. Some sample verbalizations are: "I count." ... "I'm lovable." ... "I deserve good things in my life." ... "I deserve to be good to myself."

5. **Make an Interest List.**

Patients write down their interests, beliefs, values, sources of fun and pleasure.

6. **Help patients experience control over their own being.**

Have them take walks. While walking, they vary their pace from slow to quick to a comfortable stride. Consciously and deliberately they experiment with controlling their own pace and rhythm.

7. **Encourage patients to take time for themselves.**

Instruct them to be alone and take quiet time for themselves on a daily basis. Suggested uses of this time may be to read, do crossword puzzles, meditate, do relaxation techniques, daydream, or reflect.

To help adult children see the totality of their life experience, explore with them what their painful events in the past have taught and given them now. Assist them in owning the resultant strengths they have developed to tackle, overcome, and survive difficulties and persevere. Many adult children, as children, were robbed early of their innocence, lightness, and ability to play. At a young age they took on adult responsibilities such as working outside the home, parenting younger siblings, or taking charge of the household chores. As a result, however, they learned to be responsible, hardworking, and diligent. Many adult children learned how to problem-solve objective tasks, take the initiative, take independent action, be perceptive and sensitive to others, and be highly organized. Specifically iterate with the adult children the attributes particular to them.

Explore with patients the positives they received in their childhood. No matter how severe the pain and trauma, they were cared for in some ways. Encourage patients to identify things given to them by their parents, no matter how basic: food, shelter, clothing, the sperm and egg that created them. Direct them to look outside of their family of origin to the people who were there for them in times of need or want. In session, have the *adult child write letters to these people expressing gratitude* for their availability, nurturing, caring, support, attention, or role modeling. The letters are not intended to be mailed. The value of this exercise is intensified if the letters are read aloud in the therapy session.

Aid patients in breaking the myths they hold about their parents. Have them *list at least ten events, experiences, or characteristics that have helped to shape who each parent is. Have them research their parents and family of origin. Encourage them to gather data about their parents' relationships with their family of origin.* Seeing this information in black and white has many benefits. It separates and helps individuate adult children from their parents. They gain an awareness of how the pain, trauma, and dysfunctional behavior has been filtered down through generations. They know not only what their parents gave or didn't give to them, but also what their parents were *capable* of giving. They also know what their parents received or didn't receive from their respective parents. Adult children can then view the bigger picture, the legacy handed to their parents from their grandparents, and the legacy they now have the power to stop.

In dispelling some of the myths and seeing where they and their parents have come from, these patients can open themselves to being able to have greater empathy and understanding for who their parents are. Thus, they let go of some more of their pent-up anger.

STAGE SIX — FORGIVENESS

Characteristics and Symptomatology
Of the FORGIVENESS Stage

Adult children in the **FORGIVENESS** stage are in their final stage of healing. They have acquired the ability to see how their past traumas fit into the wholeness of their lives. They know that they are more and have experienced more than only traumas. They have an understanding that unhappy and difficult events happened to them, but these events are not them and need not define who they are. Just as they don't use their troubled past to excuse themselves or their behavior, they no longer blame others or deflect responsibility for themselves, their lives, or their personhood on to others. They are able to put the players of their childhood into a balanced perspective.

They know and can accept that the people who hurt them are more than painful deeds perpetrated upon the adult child. They allow themselves to see the totality of these people, not just their ugliness, weaknesses, and faults. They can also realistically see the part they themselves played in their own histories. They embrace their childhood and their inner child with feelings of compassion, forgiveness, and love.

In this final stage, adult children have a keener knowledge of and cherish the totality of who they are. They feel deserving and worthy of getting their needs met, of having joy in their lives, and of being loved. They feel comfortable with giving and receiving love, affection, and intimacy.

Tasks to Accomplish
In the FORGIVENESS Stage

The fundamental task of the **FORGIVENESS** stage is for patients to feel confident that they have the skills, strengths, and resources to live their lives as they wish to live them. They regain trust in their own feelings and perceptions. They willingly take stock of and own all of who they are — their strengths and weaknesses, their past and goals. They reach full awareness of self-determination versus acting or feeling the victim of others or events. They welcome the responsibility of their present-day lives and the current choices that they make. They learn further acceptance of what *is*, rather than perseveration of what *should* be.

They establish an inner balance. They become more aware of what works for them and what doesn't. In doing so, they become more sure of themselves and make greater use of the tools that bring manageability into their lives. They learn to believe in themselves and to utilize this self-worth as a motivational force to expand themselves. They develop a willingness and determination to create and follow through on goals and tasks. As a result of achieving an inner balance, they allow themselves to experience real interpersonal, emotional intimacy with clearly defined boundaries.

The healing that requires the support, structure, and direction of a therapeutic setting comes to an end during the **FORGIVENESS** stage. Therefore, the final task of this stage is to terminate therapy.

Interventions to Implement
In the FORGIVENESS Stage

The interventions of the **FORGIVENESS** stage are focused on adult children incorporating and integrating all that they have learned and all the changes they have made up to this point. This is unlike the prior stages of healing where the purpose of the interventions were to open doors of awareness or to acquire new skills.

The therapist is less in control and much less directive. His or her role is more passive so patients can rely on their own survival tools, self-care skills, problem-solving abilities, feelings, and perceptions. The therapist says little, does not provide answers, and only presents questions that assist the adult child in self-exploration. The therapist acts as a consultant. He or she *mirrors for the adult child the confidence that the adult child is capable of* — especially when the adult child feels he or she is floundering.

Every opportunity is seized by the therapist to have the adult children trust, depend on, and use their internal resources. Conscious effort is made to give validation of and permission for the full range and spectrum of feelings. The therapist strives to *reinforce adult children's independence.* The therapist *further encourages patients to reclaim their personal power,* as well as recognizing the impact they have on their own lives.

The therapist assists patients in fully discovering what their needs are, how it feels to freely express them, and ways in which their needs can be met. Patients tune-in to themselves and take the time to feel their feelings and acknowledge their needs at that moment. They pose the following questions to themselves: *Can I fulfill my needs on my own? . . . Do I need help? . . . If I need help, where and from whom can I realistically get it?* They then embolden themselves to utilize their *Present Resource List* (see **VYING FOR CONTROL** stage, page 61) and ask directly for the help they require in meeting their needs.

At this stage of the healing process, adult children have a realistic picture of their family of origin. They see the good and the bad, the strengths and the weaknesses, what their families are capable of giving and what they are incapable of giving. If the adult child is willing and feels a desire to do so, *the therapist can help him or her make amends with one, some, or all of his or her family of origin.* The following techniques can be used in asking for forgiveness for what the adult child did or for offering forgiveness to others for deeds done to the adult child.

1. Patients can write a *letter* — with the intent of mailing it or not — to the person they wish to express their forgiveness to.

2. Patients can express forgiveness through *action.* They can demonstrate their sentiments by doing things for the person they forgive or for the person from whom they seek forgiveness. For instance, if they didn't lend support to a sibling in the past, how can they show their support today? If they didn't display compassion to a friend in the past, how can they show it today?

3. If the person involved in the forgiveness is emotionally or physically unavailable, adult children can verbalize their feelings through *role-play in session.* They can act out the anticipated responses of the person, as well as express what is true for themselves.

4. *If the person involved in the forgiveness is deceased, they can perform a ritual* — either in or out of the session — to fulfill their need to make amends. This could be accomplished by going to the grave site and speaking there, as if to the person. Or they could write their personal version of the deceased person's eulogy.

5. If adult children want to *express forgiveness directly, face-to-face,* it is suggested that they practice the anticipated verbal dialogue in session. Explored would be their expectations, their true purpose, and their motives. The clearer they are about what they want to accomplish, the more successful they will be regarding their own healing.

6. *Adult children can approach the person with whom they wish to make amends with love that is free from judgment or blame.* In doing so, they allow themselves

to open up their heart-space. They become intrinsically aware of their personal strength and their ability to keep themselves safe. They no longer feel vulnerable to any real or imagined hurt the person may try to inflict.

Making amends and expressing forgiveness of others are ways of putting a closure on the past. But they are not the only ways, and they are not vital in order for adult children to experience healing. Many adult children are happy with themselves and their lives while being unable or disinclined to absolve the persons who hurt them. What is critical is that the adult children forgive themselves.

Patients in the FORGIVENESS stage are ready to and need to take the helm and determine the use of their therapeutic milieu. They tend to want to use the therapeutic session to look at and work through immediate and current stressors. In taking the lead by exploring with the therapist their own approach to situations, the choices they see, their decision to either live with or resolve the stress, and the possible consequences they can anticipate to the actions they take, adult children develop self-confidence and self-reliance. The problem-solving process is the focus, not the problem itself, nor the content of the choice they make.

As these patients near termination of therapy, they not only take more control of the direction and content of their sessions, but of the frequency of the therapeutic contacts as well. The therapist fosters in the adult child a greater independence from therapy. The sessions may decrease to every other week, to every three weeks, then to once a month. Therapy terminates gradually, not abruptly. Matching the adult child's desired pace, it fades in intensity and frequency. How the therapy ends is an intervention in itself. It can have an extremely positive impact on the adult child to end the therapeutic relationship with closeness, caring, support, and his or her self-esteem intact. For many adult children, ending a relationship in such a loving way will be a first-time experience, and therefore very powerful.

CHAPTER FOUR

Adjunctive Therapies
In a Group Format

Generally, a supportive group experience can be beneficial for anyone in any kind of emotional pain. Each member can gain comfort in knowing he or she is not alone and is not the only one going through this type of turmoil. The group provides its members feedback, validation, and comfort. It can exemplify, through the diversity of its membership, the various stages of healing, thus bringing hope to its participants. It is a safe place to open up to others, give to others, and receive. Through sharing and feeling the commonality of their situations, an uncommon bond develops between group members.

For adult children of alcoholics specifically, the benefits of participating in a group can be enormous. Adult children suffer from seeing themselves as "terminally unique" and possess intense feelings of isolation. The secrecy rules they learned from their family of origin (don't talk, don't feel, and so on) reinforce these perceptions. Their emotional solitude can lead to distortions and mistrust of their views of the world and reality. They fear if they feel anything, let alone something different than what others feel, they must be crazy. The group process helps to dispel these fears and misperceptions.

Many adult children trust others even less than they trust themselves. They may maintain an impenetrable wall in order to keep distance between themselves and the assumed hurtful world and the people in it. Individual therapy can act as a first step for them in learning trust, support, and validation. A group expands that experience, offering the adult child peers with whom to be vulnerable and to share.

A group can be a very powerful catalyst for change. Hearing others' stories and feelings tends to jog and trigger the emotions and memories the listener may have long repressed or denied. Witnessing another's courage can embolden one to face, own, and deal with one's own difficult issues. The new-found awareness that others have faced similar dilemmas and made similar choices can help dispel self-blame. Groups can provide hope. Adult children's faith and optimism can grow from seeing others who have been where they are now, and knowing that those others have successfully moved closer to healing. Faith and optimism can also come from recognizing that a person is dealing with an issue that the adult child has already conquered. Groups foster the reinforcement of the process of change.

This chapter will present three kinds of group formats that these patients can participate in and benefit from. These are (1) the anonymous or Twelve Step programs, (2) group psychotherapy, and (3) therapeutic workshops.

ANONYMOUS OR TWELVE STEP GROUPS

The Twelve Step groups are all part of an international network of nonprofit, peer support groups directed at helping addicts, and the family and friends of addicts. The groups are free of charge. They are usually offered seven days a week at various times day and night. Participants are encouraged to attend as many meetings in a day or week as they wish. The commitment to attend meetings and "work the program," which means to apply what is learned at the meetings and work toward recovery, is strictly up to each participant.

The groups are broken down and labeled according to the role of the person, the relationship to the addiction, or the nature of the addiction. The following is a sample list of these groups: Alcoholics Anonymous (AA) for alcoholics; Narcotics Anonymous (NA) for drug addicts; Overeaters Anonymous (OA) for those with eating disorders; Al-Anon for friends and relatives of an alcoholic; Nar-Anon for friends and relatives of a drug addict; Alateen for teenage children of an alcoholic; Alatot for young children of an alcoholic; ACOA or ACA for adult children of alcoholics; and Co-Dependents Anonymous (CoDA) for people who are codependent. All of these groups are based on the same principles, beliefs, tenets, approaches, and methodologies in order to achieve recovery. They all perceive anonymity and confidentiality as the foundation to the success of the program.

Overall, the Twelve Step program has proved to be a vital asset to the advancement of healing. The members of each particular group have all been through similar circumstances and carry similar emotional burdens. The support they provide each other goes way beyond the meeting walls. At the end of each meeting, the participants are encouraged to socialize and exchange telephone numbers. They are also encouraged to have sponsors who help them work specific aspects of their programs. They become available to each other for friendship, program wisdom, and help through personal and family crises.

Twelve Step program philosophy does not subscribe to individual psychotherapy or psychology as a means to recovery. It is not a system with which the therapist formally interacts, although it is highly recommended that therapists do attend meetings independent of their patients. It is really through attendance that the therapist can begin to understand the program and ascertain the value of the meetings. Twelve Step meetings often generate much self-awareness and introspection for its participants. These newly conscious insights are then available to understand, process, work through, or act as a means to deeper issues through the individual psychotherapeutic milieu.

GROUP PSYCHOTHERAPY

Group psychotherapy is led by an objective, trained professional, whose skill facilitates connections between each participant's content and process. The group uses its membership to express and test out the impact of their full range of emotions, develop intimacy skills, establish personal identities, increase their sense of self-worth, and develop and test interpersonal boundaries. The leader keeps the group focused and on task, ensuring the continual identification and exploration of pertinent and relevant therapeutic issues.

The average, effective size for a therapy group is eight participants. A small group allows for group cohesion and bonding, which promotes trust, closeness, and honest disclosure. This trust takes the shape of confidence within each member of the group. It becomes the building block upon which group member relationships are established. The group's supportive, safe, and structured environment provides a permissible forum in which to experiment with and try out new interpersonal behaviors. A positive group experience, on the whole, constructs a pathway of sharing that generalizes into the participants' personal lives.

Another factor that kindles the trust level is the use of a group attendance contract. It is suggested that the group run for a finite period, optimally ten to twelve weeks. Each group member makes a promise to the group leader and other members to attend for the duration. At the end of the contractual period, the group can elect to continue or disband. The contract acts as a demonstration of responsibility and commitment — to oneself, the group, the group members, and one's own healing process.

THERAPEUTIC WORKSHOPS

A therapeutic workshop is a one-time, intensive group experience that is both experiential and educational. Because of its therapeutic nature and the individual, personal, and emotional risks involved, it is most effective when it is relatively small — no more than twenty-five participants. Two therapists co-leading the workshop is also suggested (a workshop can be draining for one therapist to conduct alone). Additionally, two sets of human senses allow for greater awareness of the workshop's process so less is unattended to, missed, or unobserved.

It has been our experience that bringing together a group of adult children who are in similar stages of their healing process can catapult them into further stages of healing. The dynamics and intensity of a workshop can trigger awareness and healing that might have taken four to six individual therapy sessions to accomplish. Additionally, besides support, the workshop provides role modeling, identification through commonly shared experiences, feedback, and validation. By definition, it allows for unloading difficult, emotional information and is a place for the participants to learn more effective options and more congruent choices while gaining a clearer picture of their personal path to healing.

Framework for Creating a Workshop

In planning a therapeutic workshop, therapists need to consider the common emotional struggles and behavioral patterns they wish to address. From these commonalities, the therapists draw the focus and theme of their workshop. We have tended to use therapeutic workshops to increase the participants' awareness of their relationships with, and within, their family of origin, and the impact this has had on their present relationships. From this standpoint, the therapists would choose a specific topic depending on the needs of their current adult children patients. These have included, but have not been limited to intimacy, boundaries, identity, control, marital/couple roles, family roles, communication patterns, self-worth, and forgiveness.

A desirable milieu contributes to the success of a workshop, as much as does the theme and therapeutic structure. A nurturing atmosphere sets the tone for free disclosure and sharing of important information. Therefore, it is helpful for the participants if the therapists create a setting as relaxed, comfortable, and informal as possible. Food soothes the soul and shows attention to basic needs. Try to provide food that fosters calmness, clear thinking, and nourishment such as fruit juices, herbal teas, whole grain muffins, or trail mix. Encourage participants to wear loose-fitting, casual clothing so they can feel free of physical restriction. Offer various forms of seating arrangements (floor, floor pillows, chairs) as well as make clear that participants can move and stretch if need be. Try to ensure that bathroom facilities are convenient and accessible. Lastly, at the onset of the workshop, tell the participants the workshop's rules, anticipated break times, and the location of basic conveniences. This makes the workshop predictable, which facilitates safety and security in the group.

The following is a general framework upon which therapists can build on to create their own individual and specific workshops.

1. Introduction

Explained is the purpose of the workshop, its direction, and goals.

2. Workshop Rules

Stressed is the need for confidentiality, mutual respect, and a nonjudgmental attitude. The group is instructed to introduce themselves by their first names only.

3. Workshop Format

The participants are informed of break times; availability and location of food, drink, and bathrooms; organization of the workshop; and how the workshop material will be presented. We have found that a running time of three hours is optimum. Less time is not enough to cover all the necessary information and to facilitate experiential learning. More time, and the participants become too tired and lose interest.

4. *Joining*

Several exercises are conducted. The first is some form of inner quieting exercise to help each participant connect with him- or herself and relax. The subsequent exercise or exercises encourages group familiarity and interaction.

5. *Educational Component*

Discussed are the principles, beliefs, and factual material related to the topic of the workshop. The presentation varies: lecture, film, use of other visual aids, group discussion. The participants are invited to and encouraged to ask questions and contribute to the shared learning of the group. This piece of the workshop is important because it not only teaches the participants something of value, but also builds further group cohesion in a nonthreatening way. The group's cohesion, trust, and comfort level contributes to the effectiveness of any experiential exercises done later in the workshop.

6. *Break*

This is usually the midpoint of the workshop. A suggested amount for break time is fifteen minutes.

7. *Experiential Component*

This is an opportunity for the participants to grow from and experience on a personal level the material shared and learned in the first half of the workshop. It is very structured and is directed by the therapists. Breaking the large group into several small groups and then resuming the large group has been found to increase the depth and intimacy of the exercises.

8. *Closure*

The group forms a circle. Participants, including the therapists, are given the opportunity to summarize their thoughts, reflect on their experience, and share what they have learned or gained. The participants are asked to offer feedback as to their perceptions of the workshop: what they found favorable as well as suggestions for improvement.

CONCLUSION

A therapeutic group experience provides common benefits regardless of its form or milieu. The sharing of similar, familiar circumstances creates an atmosphere of trust and mutuality that furthers the self-acceptance of its participants. The group structure also affords a network of support, nurturing, giving, and receiving. When adult children utilize the group modality in conjunction with individual psychotherapy, they tend to move more rapidly through the stages of healing. In addition, therapeutic groups assist the psychotherapist. The energy and power generated by these groups enhance the therapist's therapeutic knowledge of and sensitivity to the needs of their adult children patients.

CHAPTER FIVE

General Therapeutic Guidelines

Adult children of alcoholics have special clinical needs. It is advantageous to both the patient and the therapist for the therapist to be actively cognizant of the impact that his or her choice of attitude, role, pace, and style has on the outcome of treatment. It is important to be aware of successful options as well as what may impede the therapeutic process. This chapter details basic areas and themes of consideration for therapists to hold in the forefront of their work throughout the stages of healing. It is our hope that these general guidelines will assist therapists in experiencing the unique challenge of working with adult children as fluid and ever-changing, rather than as feeling stuck by unknown obstacles.

Long-Term Therapy

The healing process for adult children does not occur with the use of brief, short-term therapy. It is a long-term commitment for both the therapist and the patient. These patients have had a series of traumas, many from as far back as infancy. Each current pain, each behavior that works against them today is heavily weighted and reinforced by the past.

Treatment is a lengthy continuum of identifying and working through past situations and feelings. After confronting and emotionally rewriting the past, adult children can then opt for more fulfilling choices in the present. A woman, physically abused by her father as a child, must own, express, and let go of her rage, fear, and sadness before she can trust and feel safe in an intimate relationship as an adult. A man with low self-worth, who places others' needs and feelings before his own, must undo the old negative beliefs about himself and grow to feel deserving, before receiving and having balance in a relationship today. A woman who has always seen herself as a victim must go back to regain her power and release self-blame, in order to take charge and take control of her life today.

It all takes time. It all takes patience. The therapist needs to know this before embarking on the therapeutic journey with an adult child.

An additional factor to the long-term nature of the therapeutic relationship is the development of a strong bond of caring between the therapist and the patient. Because of the patient's level of neediness, an unfortunate, common pitfall is the fostering of dependency upon the therapist; the therapist can lose sight of the necessary therapeutic boundary. If the therapist is too available or too controlling, the patient can receive the message that he or she does not have the ability to manage his or her own life effectively. Although in the initial stage the adult child may need guidance and direction, always treat the patient with respect and overt trust in his or her adult wisdom. Give consistent messages that the patient is in charge of his or her life and choices. From the onset of therapy, know that the ultimate goal is independence and individuation. Find the balance between support and fostering independence. Provide nurturance along with trust and assurance in the patient's capabilities.

Identification with Being
An Adult Child of an Alcoholic

When adult children of alcoholics learn about alcoholism and the impact it has on the family, they experience a great deal of relief. A sense of grounding occurs in knowing there is a cause, a reason to their reality. It is validating and reassuring to know they are not alone, they are not crazy, they are not bad, and they are not to blame.

Identification with being a child of an alcoholic, however, is not the be all and end all to healing. It is not a label, an excuse, or a tool for adult children to use to deflect from taking responsibility for their lives, themselves, their decisions, or their relationships. It is unfortunate that many of these patients get stuck in this place and don't move on (see **VYING FOR CONTROL** stage, Chapter Three). Making the emotional and intellectual connection that he or she is a child of an alcoholic can provide the patient with an initial safety float. The therapist needs to keep in mind, though, that the adult child still needs to learn how to swim.

Multi-Faceted Therapeutic Approach

It is our opinion that it's detrimental to the healing process for therapists to limit their view of their patients to their emotional makeup alone. To acknowledge the many dimensions of a person — heredity, physiology, spirituality, and psyche — expands the therapist's mind and creativity, and furthers the patient's change and healing. In accepting people's multi-dimensional nature, therapists need to be flexible and diverse in their therapeutic approach and means of intervention. Rather than possibly being overwhelmed by the complexity of human beings, therapists can broaden their abilities by freeing up and trusting their creative instincts. We would like to encourage therapists to intellectually stretch, to use verbal as well as nonverbal techniques, to be inventive and intuitively resourceful.

Multiple Therapeutic Milieus

Individual psychotherapy is only one part of the healing process for adult children of alcoholics. The therapist must not be the patient's sole lifeline, nor his or her sole vehicle for change. As a therapist, be supportive and encouraging of the patient's use of adjunctive therapies, as opposed to being competitive with other milieus or possessive of the patient and his or her treatment. At appropriate points in the healing process, suggest the patient begin participation in one or more of the following: Al-Anon; ACA or ACOA; Co-DA; group therapy; an intensive therapeutic weekend; family therapy; couple's therapy; a therapeutic workshop; or a community workshop (see Chapter Four for specific guidelines for this decision). If the patient seeks an additional therapeutic milieu in order to enhance his or her growth, maintenance of contact between therapists helps keep therapeutic messages consistent and presents a team approach in working with the adult child.

Working from the Patient's Vantage Point

Each adult child's path of recovery is individual and unique. As a therapist, try not to get fixed in thinking there is only one road, one modality, one solution. Act as a role model of flexibility for the patient. When an approach, an intervention, or a concept doesn't seem to work, try something else, try something new; individualize the format, setting, style, and frequency of sessions to suit and to be effective for that particular patient.

Honor not only what assists the healing, but also the times when the adult child appears stuck or choosing against progress or change. There is a reason for his or her entrenchment. Many adult children of alcoholics will not give something up until they know they have something definite to replace it with. They may not yet feel safe enough to move on. They may not trust themselves, therapy, or the therapist enough to try on a new unfamiliar behavior and risk giving up a comfortable, though negative, pattern.

Providing Direction

In the beginning stages of healing, it is necessary for therapists to be directive, take the helm, and lead the therapeutic process. They need to provide structure within the sessions in order to be concrete and active in their interventions and statements to the adult child. At times, the therapist will take on the role of teacher, educating patients about the disease concept of alcoholism and the impact alcoholism has on the family. At other times, the therapist will act as a guide on the healing path, bringing patients back on to the therapeutic track when they stray.

Frequently, adult children create or put up a smoke screen of crises to distract themselves or to avoid dealing with primary issues. The therapist then leads patients back into refocusing on their therapeutic work. Because of the difficulty of the information and due to their own emotional defense systems, adult children tend to report events in their lives with emotional detachment. The therapist directs and steers patients into experiencing the feelings — not just talking about them.

Providing Validation

At every realistic opportunity, affirm, validate, confirm, and support adult children's feelings, opinions, and perceptions. Provide reality testing and feedback to their choices and decisions. Balance this, however, with handing the patients' lives over to them. Be sure to give them choices in all possible moments and to give them the responsibility for the choices they make. It is a strong temptation to cross that line from being directive to parental. It is imperative that the therapist be careful not to give advice, make decisions for patients, deny or judge patients' feelings, or minimize patients' perception of their experiences. In doing any of these, the therapist can duplicate patients' dysfunctional familial patterns, discount patients' integrity, and reinforce such self-defeating beliefs as *I don't know better.... I don't count.... Other people control my life. ... I must be crazy.*

The therapist's basic trust in the patient facilitates the adult child's trust in him- or herself. For adult children, the therapist may be the first person who has ever believed they have the wisdom to take charge of their own lives. The therapist may be the first person to communicate to them that they truly deserve to be happy and have their needs met. The therapist's trust that they can do it — change, integrate, love, heal — is in itself a powerful intervention tool.

An additional part of providing validation is not just affirming the patients' personhood, but their therapeutic progress as well. Two typical adult child traits work against them: the need to do everything perfectly, and the perception of the world in dichotomous extremes — all-or-nothing, all-black-or-all-white. These traits act as a funnel into which neutral information is put in, and from which emotionally self-denigrating beliefs come out. In therapy this translates into impatience: "I want to be totally healed by next week, and if I am not, I am a total failure as a patient." Frustration: "I have been in therapy six months, done everything you told me to do, and I still hurt. I must be a bad person and not deserve to get better." Anger mixed with blame: "It's all your fault. I didn't feel this pain before I came into therapy. If you were a better therapist, I would be all healed by now. Any happiness I may have isn't worth feeling if it's going to feel this bad."

These are just a few examples of how adult children may try to negate or discount their own growth. They tend to interpret their emotional pain as punishment or reinforcement that they are truly not enough, that nothing they do is good enough. How these traits manifest are as diverse as the patients themselves, but manifest they do.

To help circumvent these traits and to help adult children deal with them, the therapist directly and overtly points out, celebrates, commends, and notes every and any change or positive step the patient makes. Let no progress go unnoticed. Assist patients in refocusing on what they have done; reinforce to them the courage they have demonstrated; exemplify the clear perceptions and wisdom they have already shown.

Painting a Balanced Picture

Because of the level and extent of emotional trauma, there is much focus in the therapeutic sessions on the pain, weaknesses, and deprivation experienced by adult children from childhood through the present day. The empathetic therapist is vulnerable to adult children's dichotomous thinking and may be tempted to side with their sad and angry feelings against their parents. As a therapist, it is imperative to stay neutral. Understand that there are beautiful aspects to the patient; therefore, the therapist has concrete proof that positives came out of the adult child's family of origin as well.

Adult children of alcoholics also tend to judge their parents dichotomously: one good parent (the sober parent, if there was one), and one bad parent (the alcoholic). Be sensitive to the fact that this perception is taken to extremes. The patient may idealize the sober parent, having difficulty assigning any human frailties or faults to him or her. The patient may also resist acknowledging any positive traits in the alcoholic parent. Adult children establish these dichotomous perceptions as part of their emotional defense repertoire. As with all of adult children's defenses, the therapist needs to respect them and the purpose they hold for patients. As is appropriate, gently and slowly assist patients in seeing the totality of each parent. As an aside, it is usually easier for adult children to assign positive attributes to the alcoholic parent than it is to conceive of the sober parent having negative attributes or weaknesses. Adult children can accept and love the totality of themselves only after seeing more balance within their parents.

Availability

Particularly in the beginning stages of the healing process, and during more stressful periods of emotional growth, adult children of alcoholics tend to reach out to their therapist for support, strength, and guidance outside of the therapeutic session. This is appropriate and predictable. Being available for telephone contact helps them build trust, gives them a covert message of permission to ask to get their needs met, lets them know they are not alone, and communicates that they count and that their feelings matter. Conversely, the therapist needs to reinforce that they are not and cannot be the patient's sole resource. The therapist is not a substitute for friends, family members, a support group, or a program sponsor. Encourage patients to utilize the total network of support available to them.

Transferential Issues

An inevitable result of the potent combination of adult children's emotional makeup, traumatic history, and the long-term nature of their therapy is the therapist facing feelings and reactions that the adult child has for him or her. These transferential responses can take on various forms. The following are a few examples of how the transference may behaviorally be expressed, the reason behind the behavior, and some options to deal with it in a way that benefits both the patient and the therapist.

Because of their issues surrounding trust, adult children of alcoholics may try to distance themselves emotionally and physically from the therapist as they begin to be vulnerable and disclose in session. The overt behavior may look like any of the following:

- Dropping out of therapy.
- Not following through on between-session tasks.

- Repetitive lateness.
- A pattern of forgetting the time or date of the scheduled therapy session.

Also, because of trust issues, the opposite reaction may occur. Some adult children will feel they need to ingratiate themselves with the therapist in order to maintain the therapeutic relationship. The clues to this internal process would be:

- Offering presents to the therapist.
- Overcompliance with in-session and out-of-session therapy tasks.
- Withholding feelings or personal history for fear of rejection if the information was shared.

As has been discussed, many adult children of alcoholics feel a parental void. They are starved for nurturance, attention, direction, and validation. What they are so hungry for is obviously a part of what is offered and available through therapy. Some patients will confuse and misunderstand the therapeutic relationship and will try to fill their parenting needs through it. They will attempt to become overinvolved with the therapist, will foster a dependency, and will try to get as much contact with the therapist as possible, both by phone and in person. They will assign feelings and motivations to the therapist of a personal nature, rather than of a professional one, such as "We're friends." . . . "I'm more than just one of his patients." Again, in response, the therapist must define and reinforce interpersonal and therapeutic boundaries.

As patients' feelings shift from self-blame to externalizing their anger, the anger will be expressed in the therapy session, most often directly at the therapist. The therapist is an appropriate and safe receptacle for the anger. In fact, getting angry with the therapist is a real sign of trust in the therapist and therapeutic process. Feeling the anger and experiencing the release of anger within the therapy session are beginning steps to risking direct confrontation with the sources of the patient's negative feelings in his or her personal life.

In response to any form of transference, the first step is to notice and be aware of the adult child's needs and process. As with any behavior, there are reasons and justifications for the transference. Be accepting and respectful of the adult child and his or her individuality and choices. Concurrently, it is important that the therapist deal directly with the patient and discuss the behavioral manifestations of the transference. Give feedback, clearly define therapeutic boundaries, and provide concrete rules and guidelines. Above all, the therapist need not take these behaviors or their underlying feelings personally. They are the patient's issues and should not become the therapist's issues. In recognizing transference and the role it plays for the adult child, the therapist can utilize it as a stepping stone in the adult child's growth and healing.

Parents — Internal and Real

Many adult children of alcoholics have two sets of "parents." One set is the parents they perceive themselves to have, that they carry in their hearts and in their heads. The other set is the actual flesh-and-blood people. Adult children carry within them all the unresolved needs that their real parents have not met, along with the hope that their childhood needs will one day be fulfilled. They perceive their internal parents as capable of being all that they want them to be. They believe they have the power to change the relationship between themselves and their real parents. They feel they can mold their real parents into being the internal parents they hold on to so dearly. If they are not yet successful in causing this change to occur, they will vacillate between two points of view: either they have not yet found the right key to facilitate the metamorphosis, or they in fact feel they are not deserving of having their most basic emotional needs met. In both perspectives, they may feel totally responsible for the balance and nature of the relationship. If they are not getting their needs met, it is their fault, their blame, their shame.

A major step in the healing process involves coming to terms with their internal parents. The therapist assists them in dealing with the specific issues, needs, and expectations surrounding both their internal and real parents. Fostered is the awareness and acceptance of who their parents really are, that their parents may never change, and that it isn't their responsibility to make that change happen. Reinforced is the new belief that it's not that they don't deserve to get their needs met, it's only that their parents are incapable of giving them what they so desperately want and need. Rather than futilely trying to change their parents' behavior, these patients can learn to have a different emotional response to their parents' behavior.

In seeing and accepting their parents for who they are, they are able to let their parents go as a dominant force in their lives. They can release the painful and frustrating hope that their parents will one day love them the way they want their parents to love them. Instead, they can embrace themselves and their needs as something valuable and warranted. They can actively seek to get their needs met by people capable of meeting them.

CHAPTER SIX

Therapist Self-Care

It is our perception that conducting psychotherapy is stressful, difficult, and draining no matter who the specific population is. Therapists are skilled caretakers of others, but are usually just as skilled at neglecting themselves. They boast and lecture about the value of therapy, play, relaxation, and being honest with oneself, but conduct their lives as if those things pertain to everyone except them. We would like to suggest what may seem like a radical concept: the therapists' clarity, health, state of mind, sense of self-worth, and well being are just as valuable as those to whom they devote their professional lives. We offer this chapter to the person inside the therapist suit.

Practicing Patience

Psychotherapy with adult children of alcoholics is a long-term process. Given how resourceful these patients are, if it was quick and easy they would read their way into healing and not need a trained professional. As a therapist, take the pressure off yourself. Recognize an adult child's recovery is a series of progressions and regressions. As with any population, their healing occurs at a personal pace. There are no "right" time frames or earmarks for recovery. The patient, not the therapist, is in charge of his or her life, decisions, and how therapy is used. You can offer the tools and show the path, but you can't force their implementation or coerce a person into changing course.

Balancing Your Caseload

Having an area of specialization can be beneficial for therapists, their business, and their patients. But it can also be very taxing to work with one issue exclusively, particularly the impact of alcoholism. It can create tunnel vision, stunt the therapist's creativity, and produce feelings of boredom, frustration, or cynicism. Help to keep yourself and the world in perspective by working with various presenting problems and populations.

Emotional Reactions and Identification

Adult children of alcoholics have typically experienced more trauma than the average patient that is generally seen in an outpatient private practice. It is usual to hear histories riddled with sexual abuse, emotional abuse, physical abuse, and neglect. It is painful and sad to hear and feel what they have survived. In reaction, you may feel a range of emotions toward the patient and his or her family.

Perhaps you are not just responding to the patient's pain, but are identifying with an issue that he or she is grappling with, an issue unresolved for yourself. This is not uncommon and can happen whether you are an adult child of an alcoholic or not. Much of an adult child's emotional material can overlap with the emotional material of those whose lives are less traumatic.

It is important as an effective therapist to accept and acknowledge your personal responses. Take whatever measures you can in order to not work alone or in a vacuum. Provide yourself with a person with whom you can release the hurt, gain support, and work on your own issues. This can be a professional peer, a professional peer group, or your own therapist. If you don't engage in some formal forum for introspection, both you and your patients will suffer. Both of you will be stuck in the areas of your own issues.

Unfortunately, many therapists, particularly once they are established and actively working in the field, resist engaging in their own psychotherapy. They espouse the righteousness of therapy and its benefits to everyone but themselves. It is our perception that our profession, professional schools, and training arenas hold a negative opinion of those who seek psychotherapy. Even the language we use reflects the viewpoint that people who seek help are thought of as "less" than people who don't. They have "problems," "weaknesses," "difficulties." As professionals, we talk about pathology, dysfunction, sickness, and diagnostic labels. If at some level we judge our patients for needing or seeking therapy, then it follows that we would have resistance to being in therapy ourselves.

Boundaries

Most adult children of alcoholics who therapists see professionally seem to have a bottomless, empty pit within them that bespeaks their plethora of unfulfilled and unmet needs, wants, and desires. These patients can appear directionless, helpless, and extremely needy. These qualities and personality traits may play on the sympathetic impulses of the therapist. There may be a very strong draw to act as caretaker, nurturer, or rescuer. Know that to have any or even overwhelming emotional reactions to these people is usual. It is how these emotional reactions are expressed that indicates ethical behavior and healthy psychotherapy.

When we, as therapists, act on our overprotective or parental impulses, we are acting out of our own personal needs and not out of consideration as to what would be in the best interest of our patients. Remember to practice patience and professional, emotional distancing. Trust in your patients' need to be where they are, not where you want them to be. Keep in the forefront that you are doing the best you can.

There are additional important boundaries beyond those between therapist and patient. These are between the work role of therapist and your personal life, and between yourself and the people in your personal life. Allow yourself to disengage from your work. Remember that you are more than a therapist. Develop hobbies and interests. Make time for yourself. Give yourself permission to say no to others. Set appropriate limits on yourself, and on the imposition others may place on your life. Create your own safe place and territory. Use that safe place for your own quiet time, to regroup and be in touch with your own personhood.

Stress

Practicing psychotherapy is a stressful occupation. It is even more taxing when one seeks to help heal those affected by severe trauma, as in the case of adult children of alcoholics. As therapists, it is necessary for us to maintain our own center, to fulfill our own emotional and spiritual needs. It is only from our own filled cups that we can offer a drink of serenity, happiness, and clarity to our patients.

Maintain a balance in your life. Offset the emotional heaviness of your work with joy, lightness, creativity, spontaneity. Take time to release your tensions through exercise, meditation, massage, or simple play. Giving in such large quantities to others on a daily basis requires extra care in making sure that you also receive. Set a good example and practice what you teach your patients. Accept and embrace your own needs, weaknesses, fallibilities, and humanism. Give yourself unconditional permission to lean on at least one person in your personal life and to seek help as you desire it.

Treat yourself as the special, important person that you are.

Appendix

FACTS AND STATISTICAL DATA RELATING TO CHILDREN OF ALCOHOLICS

1. Approximately twenty-eight million Americans have an alcoholic parent, which equates to about one in every eight people. Of these twenty-eight million, seven million are under the age of eighteen years, and twenty-one million are adults.
2. Greater than 50 percent of all alcoholics have an alcoholic parent.
3. One out of three families report that alcohol is abused by one of their family members.
4. Adult children of alcoholics are at the greatest risk of becoming alcoholics or marrying alcoholics.
5. Women who abuse alcohol while pregnant give birth to children who are at higher risk of developing an attention deficit disorder or stress-related medical problem.
6. For every one thousand women who abuse alcohol while pregnant, three give birth to children suffering from Fetal Alcohol Syndrome.
7. Sons of alcoholic fathers are four times more likely to become alcoholics themselves than sons whose fathers are not alcoholic.
8. Daughters of alcoholic mothers are three times more likely to become alcoholics themselves than daughters whose mothers are not alcoholic.
9. Generally, without distinguishing by sex, children of alcoholics are four times more likely to become alcoholics themselves, than children of non-alcoholic parents.

10.   Children of alcoholics use medical and hospital services more frequently than children whose parents are not alcoholic. As compared to the general population, sons of alcoholics experience 60 percent more physical injuries, are five times more likely to be seen in a psychotherapeutic setting, and are two and one half times more likely to be diagnosed as severely ill or disabled. Daughters of alcoholics are hospitalized three and one half times more frequently than are daughters of non-alcoholic parents. Additionally, their participation in psychotherapy is three times greater than the general population. Overall, children of alcoholics (both sexes included, through age nineteen) spend an average of 7.6 days in the hospital, compared with children of non-alcoholic parents who average 5.9 days in the hospital.

SOURCES FOR STATISTICAL DATA

National Association for Children of Alcoholics. "Facts About Children of Alcoholics," 1976.

National Council on Alcoholism, Inc. "Facts on Alcoholism and Alcohol-Related Problems," rev. November, 1987.

Woodside, Migs. "Children of Alcoholics." A Report to Hugh L. Carey, Governor of New York. Children of Alcoholics Foundation, July 1982.

Woodside, Migs. "Children of Alcoholics: Helping a Vulnerable Group." Public Health Reports, vol. 103, no. 6 (Nov. - Dec. 1988): 643-647.

Suggested Reading

THE AUTHORS' TOP TEN

Our suggestions for further readings in the areas of adult children of alcoholics and codependency.

1. Beattie, Melody. *Codependent No More*. Center City, Minn.: Hazelden Educational Materials, 1987.
2. Black, Claudia. *It Will Never Happen To Me!* Denver: MAC Publishing, 1981.
3. Dwinell, Lorie and Jane Middleton-Moz. *After the Tears: Reclaiming the Personal Losses of Childhood*. Pompano Beach, Fla.: Health Communications, Inc., 1986.
4. Melody, Pia. *Facing Codependency*. San Francisco: Harper and Row, 1989.
5. Subby, Robert. *Lost in the Shuffle*. Pompano Beach, Fla.: Health Communications, Inc., 1987.
6. Wegscheider-Cruse, Sharon. *Another Chance: Hope and Health for the Alcoholic Family*. Palo Alto, Calif.: Science and Behavior Books, 1981.
7. Wegscheider-Cruse, Sharon. *Choice-Making: For Codependents, Adult Children and Spirituality Seekers*. Pompano Beach, Fla.: Health Communications, Inc., 1987.
8. Whitfield, Charles. *Healing the Child Within*. Pompano Beach, Fla.: Health Communications, Inc., 1987.
9. Woititz, Janet. *Adult Children of Alcoholics*. Pompano Beach, Fla.: Health Communications, Inc., 1983.
10. Woititz, Janet. *Struggle for Intimacy*. Pompano Beach, Fla.: Health Communications, Inc., 1985.

Index

A

Abandonment, fear of, 8-10
Abuse, significance of, in patient's history, 32
ACOA. *See* Adult Child of an Alcoholic
Adjunctive therapies, 77-81
Adult Child of an Alcoholic: definition of, 5;
    traits of, 6-23; common problems of, 27-28;
    profiles of, 28-31; guidelines in determining
    if patient is, 31-34
Affirmations, 54-55, 70
Aggressor, The, 52
Alcohol abuse in patients, 28, 34
Alcohol consumption of parents and grandparents,
    significance of, 31
Alcoholism: definition of, 5; impact on patient
    population, 2-3, 5; themes of, 2
Anecdotes, use of, 68
Anger: fear of, 8-10; nature of anger in Stage Two, 45;
    nature of anger in Stage Three, 51-52; nature of
    anger in Stage Four, 62, 64, 65; nature of anger in
    Stage Five, 66, 67
Assessment process in therapy, 27-35

B

Bataka bats, use of, 64
Behavioral patterns, identification of, 58-60
Belief systems, 5; of the adult child, 7, 8-9, 11, 22, 24;
    establishing new beliefs, 47-49; 52-53
Betrayal, fear of, 8
Boundaries. *See* Interpersonal Boundaries
Breathing, use of deep and regulated, 55, 69

C

D

J

L

M

N

O

P

Other titles that will interest you. . .

Letting Go of Shame
Understanding How Shame Affects Your Life
by Ronald Potter-Efron and Patricia Potter-Efron
Letting Go of Shame is an effective tool for helping clients identify shame and its biological, psychological, and cultural roots. Practical exercises clarify ways to take action to keep shame from disconnecting the recovering person from others. 192 pp.
Order No. 5082

Dual Disorders
Counseling Clients with
Chemical Dependency and Mental Illness
by Dennis C. Daley, M.S.W.,
Howard Moss, M.D., and Frances Campbell, M.S.N.
This guide helps chemical dependency counselors effectively treat alcoholics and addicts who also have a psychiatric disorder. It addresses the needs and concerns of these clients, increasing the counselor's awareness of the most common psychiatric disorders found in the chemically dependent. 148 pp.
Order No. 5023

Design for Growth
Twelve Steps for Adult Children
by Veronica Ray
Thought-provoking suggestions will challenge your adult child clients to personalize the issues for themselves, helping them move from denial to acceptance of the past to growth in the present. This book offers step-by-step direction useful for newcomers and as renewal for oldtimers in adult children groups. 115 pp.
Order No. 5085

For price and order information please call one of our Telephone Representatives. Ask for a free catalog describing nearly 1,500 items available through Hazelden Educational Materials.

HAZELDEN EDUCATIONAL MATERIALS

1-800-328-9000	**1-800-257-0070**	**1-612-257-4010**	**1-612-257-2195**
(Toll Free. U.S. Only)	(Toll Free. MN Only)	(AK and Outside U.S.)	(FAX)

Pleasant Valley Road • P.O. Box 176 • Center City, MN 55012-0176